THE ETRUSCANS IN THE ANCIENT WORLD

Plate I. The Liver Scrutinizer: an engraved bronze mirror from Vulci. About 400 B.C.

(By courtesy of Kohlhammer Verlag, Stuttgart)

THE ETRUSCANS

in the Ancient World

by
OTTO-WILHELM VON VACANO

Translated by
SHEILA ANN OGILVIE

INDIANA UNIVERSITY PRESS

BLOOMINGTON

Authorized translation
from the German
*Die Etrusker in der
Welt der Antike*

SECOND PRINTING 1971
Library of Congress Catalog Card Number: 60-16881
First published 1960. Copyright © Edward Arnold (Publishers) Ltd.
All Rights Reserved
First Midland Book Edition 1965 by arrangement with
St Martin's Press Incorporated
Manufactured in the United States of America
ISBN 0-253-20081-4

CONTENTS

Chapter I

LIFE GOVERNED BY RELIGION

Chapter II

ELEMENTS OF SPIRITUAL UNITY

Contents

Chapter III

LINKS WITH THE REST OF THE ANCIENT WORLD

Chapter IV

A ROYAL TOMB OF EARLY TIMES

Chapter V

THE CONFLICT WITH THE GREEKS

CHAPTER VI

ROME OR VEII

CHAPTER VII

THE END OF ETRURIA

Contents

SUMMARY OF THE STORY OF ETRURIA AND OF THE HISTORY OF ETRUSCAN RESEARCH

ILLUSTRATIONS

Plates

Drawings in the Text

Drawings in the Text

Drawings in the Text

Drawings in the Text

CHAPTER I

Life Governed by Religion

I. INTRODUCTION

B ETWEEN Florence and Rome lies the inviting land of Tuscany. This was in ancient times the home of a civilized people who possessed the art of enjoying life to the full yet at the same time were perpetually conscious of fate, death and change, and showed a strangely submissive attitude towards the powers of the underworld. The Romans called the people who created and maintained this civilization *Tusci* and *Etrusci*, but the Greeks knew them as Τυρρηνοί or Τυρσηνοί, i.e. Tyrrhenians or Tyrsenians. The name they themselves used—*Rásna, Rasenna*—was not adopted either by ancient or modern languages. Hesiod, writing about 700 B.C., speaks of the Τυρσηνοῖσιν ἀγακλειτοῖσι 'the renowned Tyrsenians', whereas Thucydides, writing in the second half of the fifth century B.C., classes them with 'barbarians'. 'Tuscan' to the Romans of later date frequently meant the same as did 'Italic' in ancient times. Finally, about A.D. 300 Arnobius was to describe Etruria from the early Christian point of view as *genetrix et mater superstitionis*, 'originator and mother of all superstition'.

Etruscan civilization had its beginnings in the ninth and eighth centuries B.C. and reached its zenith in the sixth century. Its end, or rather its assimilation into the pan-Italic civilization established by Rome, coincided with the end of the Roman Republic in the last century B.C. In 44 B.C., after Caesar's death, an Etruscan seer announced the beginning of the end of Etruscan greatness. Thus its history corresponds in time to that phase of Greece's development which had such a great influence on the intellectual and social history of Europe, the period which began with the break-up of the geometric style and the creation of the Homeric epics, continued through the period of archaic art and the age of Solon into classical times and led finally into the age of Hellenism.

The Cities of Etruria

There are two museums in Italy which house the principal Etruscan antiquities and everyone who visits Etruria should begin and end his journey in them. One is the *Museo Archeologico* in Florence with its infinitely attractive series of halls arranged according to the cities and their domains. This museum also encloses the *Giardino Archeologico* containing actual tombs collected from every part of the region. The

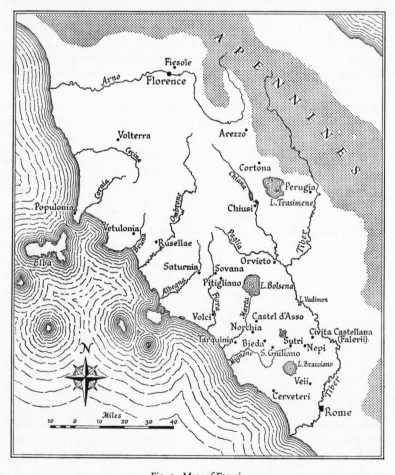

Fig. 1. Map of Etruria

other museum, in Rome, is the *Villa Giulia*, along with the *Museo Gregoriano* of the Vatican. Here the exhibits consist mainly of southern Etruscan finds, whose arrangement is a sample of the most modern display technique Italy can offer.

The towns which were once the centres of Etruscan life lie strung along the country's natural lines of communication. Inland these are the broad valleys of the Arno and the Tiber and the fertile vale of Chiana which unites them. The other route from north to south follows the coast which takes its name from the Tyrrhenians. Thus the cities lie one after the other along the inland road: Arezzo (Arretium), Cortona, Chiusi (Clusium) and Perugia (Perusia), Orvieto, Città Castellana (Falerii)[1] and desolate Veii, of which the Roman poet Propertius sang in the reign of the Emperor Augustus:

> 'Veii, thou hadst a royal crown of old,
> And in thy forum stood a throne of gold!—
> Thy walls now echo but the shepherd's horn,
> And o'er thine ashes waves the summer corn.'[2]

The coastal cities suffered frequent visitations from pirates and Saracens in the course of their history and were ravaged by malaria, emanating from the Maremma where the marshes began to spread as the Tuscan drainage system fell into ruins. These towns have now sunk into insignificance or lie isolated and completely uninhabited. Cerveteri and Tarquinii owe their recent fame to the magnificent burial-mounds and tomb-paintings which decades of archaeological work have once more exposed to view. As ports they have long been replaced by Civitavecchia.

Excavation has only recently been started on abandoned Vulci, in the hope that at last the structure and layout of an Etruscan town may be ascertained for the first time. Great white oxen with wide sweeping horns graze within the amazing walls which still enclose Rusellae, high on the mountain above the plain of Grosseto through which the Ombrone flows.

[1]The Faliscans spoke Latin with a Sabine accent, but all the evidence proves that they had close cultural and historical links with the Etruscans. Indeed some ancient witnesses regarded them as being Etruscans and it is therefore possible that they actually belonged to the Confederation of the Twelve. Their city was destroyed by the Romans in 241 B.C. and the inhabitants moved to Falerii Novi (S. Maria di Falleri).

[2]*Eleg.* IV, 10, translation from G. Dennis's 'Cities and Cemeteries of Etruria'.

Vetulonia, where the Romans believed the insignia of their magistrates originated, still survives as a little mountain village. Populonia, once a city of iron and furnaces, is now nothing but a seaside resort on the peaceful bay of Baratti, to which the restored cupola-tombs of the seventh and sixth centuries B.C. lend an additional attraction. Lastly there is Volterra, which lies in northern Tuscany on the far side of the tawny River Cecina and a good day's march inland from the sea: it has been able to retain a certain significance through its alabaster industry and is thronged with the busy life of a small provincial town.

A Land of Rich Natural Resources

This fortunate countryside, so varied in formation and vegetation, reveals its volcanic character to this day in numerous hot and cold mineral and sulphur springs, baths and delicious table waters. Formerly this soil produced good wine. The tuff[1] area stretches south from Orvieto as far as Latium, with streams which carve canyon-like gorges through the plains, the crater lake of Bolsena sparkling like silver, and the forest-clad Ciminian mountains in their age-old solitude. This is the countryside in which the Etruscans developed their peculiar rock-tomb architecture. In the cemeteries of Bieda, San Giuliano, Norchia, Castel d'Asso and of Sovana in the upper Fiora valley, are preserved hundreds of monumental tombs carved block-like out of the lava rock faces. The contours of northern Etruria on the other hand are for the most part softer, formed as they are by sedimentary deposits, while its rivers are laden with the soil and dissolved lime they wash down.

Before they had access to Sicily the Romans relied on the land of the Etruscans for their reserve granary, from which they imported grain for bread whenever their own harvest failed or suffered damage. Additional sources of great wealth were mining and a famous metal-working industry, both made possible by Elba and the Monti Metalliferi, the ore-bearing mountains of the north-west, which were the basis of the prosperity of Populonia, Volterra and Vetulonia, and by the rich mineral deposits in the woodlands of La Tolfa, which lies behind Cerveteri. The apparently inexhaustible mountain forests provided firewood for smelting the ore and timber for building temples and ships. This then was the rich soil from which Etruscan civilization

[1]Tuff—a light porous cellular rock produced by consolidation of volcanic ashes and other erupted material (translator's note).

sprang and flourished, sustained by the wealthy families and yet aiming primarily not at any expansion of power or at profit, but at dominion through religion over life and death.

Devotion to Music

Music, dancing and masks played an important role in the life of these people. The instruments they particularly favoured were the double pipes, the zither, a percussion instrument like the castanets, the short, slightly curved horn, the long, curling horn and the resonant trumpet, whose inventors they were believed to be. We learn how sweet and bemusing was the sound of the Tuscan pipes from a tale told by Aelian in his work on zoology as late as the third century of our era, when their music had long been silent.

'It is said in Etruria, where wild pigs and stags are caught with nets and dogs in the usual manner of hunters, that success is greater when music is used as an aid. I shall now relate the manner of doing this. Nets are stretched out and all kinds of traps set in position. Along comes an experienced piper. He avoids so far as possible regular melodies and loud sounds and plays the sweetest tones the double pipes can produce. In the silent solitude his airs float up to the tops of the mountains, into the gorges and thickets, into all the retreats and breeding-grounds of the game. At first when the sounds reach their ears the animals are terrified and filled with fear. But later they are irresistibly overcome by enjoyment of the music. Enraptured they abandon their young, their lairs and their familiar trails, from which they would normally be so unwilling to stray. Thus are the wild beasts of the Tyrrhenian forests gradually attracted by a powerful magic, and they draw near, bewitched by the sounds, till they fall, overpowered by the music, into the snares.' (*De natura animalium* XII, 46.)

From tombstones and urns, and above all from the gay wall-paintings of the underground burial places of Tarquinii we can learn of the lively round dances of the women, the weapon dance of the men and the passionate dance-game of youths and maidens who move and turn in couples or singly to the sound of pipes and zithers. These dances are full of dark sensual pleasure, yet at the same time restrained in a melancholy way, in spite of all their excitement and tenseness. They are the expression of a deep musicality which needs no words.

Fig. 2. Tomb painting, end of the sixth century B.C.

Livy, describing the expiation ceremonies undertaken in Rome in 364 B.C. against plague, says: 'Without singing, without even trying to express the contents of a song through gestures, the performers, who had been brought from Etruria, executed the graceful motions of Tuscan dances accompanied by a pipe.' The Etruscans called these dancers *hister*, he continues, and that is how the Romans came to call their actors *histriones*, because Roman drama grew out of these dances demonstrated on this occasion for the first time. Valerius Maximus also speaks of the *decora pernicitas*, 'the graceful agility', of the movements of those Etruscan dancers.

Music, like ritual and religious procedure, was an accompaniment to every aspect of life. The pipes were played at sacrifices and at banquets, at boxing matches and at solemn processions or displays. Indeed even bakers and cooks worked to music and it was not omitted when slaves were being flogged. Dancers and musicians had their own guilds. Their members would be summoned, like the soothsayers, to Rome whenever expiation ceremonies were performed or homage of some special kind was being offered to the gods—significant proof of the close connexion between religion and the Etruscan devotion to music.

Plate II.   The Flute-player

(*Reproduced by courtesy of Thames and Hudson from Pallottino: The Art of the Etruscans*)

Revival of Interest in the Etruscans

Lately after more than a hundred years of preliminary work by European and also for a shorter period by American archaeologists, the Etruscans have again become an object of interest to wider circles in various countries, as they once were in the first half of last century. This is demonstrated by the large number of persons who visited the great Etruscan exhibition in different capitals of Europe in 1955 and 1956. People accustomed to looking at modern and experimental art find the works of the Etruscans particularly striking and fascinating because they feel that they are not classical: it is as though the artists had used patterns discovered by the Greeks, taken them apart and then refashioned them in a fresh style. Nowadays, people greet even abstruse works of art with interest and seem ready to value novelty and oddity more highly than artistic quality.

Other things too have conspired to shed a magical glamour over the Etruscans: the difficulties associated with classification and complete knowledge of the language; the problem of origins, which gave rise to discussion even in ancient times; the unexpected encounter with works of art so numerous and glowing with the strength of primitive life, of whose existence the general public had been unaware—all this, and the attraction which the archaeologist's work has for so many people to-day. The fantastic elegance of the rich goldsmith's work in the museum show-cases intensifies curiosity as to what may still lie buried, undiscovered and unsuspected, in Tuscan soil.

Nevertheless, one can do justice to Etruscan civilization only if one attempts to see it in relation to the ancient world of which it was an integral part. Regarded in this way it may serve to open up a broader approach to an understanding of the ancients, with the richness of whose life and organization we are not yet completely familiar.

2. THE ATHRPA MIRROR

Examination of a mirror which dates from the end of the fourth century B.C. may serve as an introduction to the question of the inter-relationship of Greek and Etruscan art and at the same time afford a first glimpse of what is distinctive in the attitude of the Etruscans and their view of life.

A mirror is particularly suited to this purpose, for, while other forms of art have developed more independently, the graphic art of the

Etruscans displayed on their mirrors is so closely akin to the Hellenic art of drawing—familiar to us principally on painted vases—that a closer relationship is scarcely imaginable. Moreover the Etruscans exhibited a special partiality for mirrors so that we are justified in using them as one of the keys to the Etruscan mind.

About one thousand five hundred decorated hand-mirrors have so far emerged from Etruscan tombs into the light of day, and on the stone or earthenware lids of funerary urns the effigy of the deceased frequently appears reclining in state, a mirror in his hand.

Souls and Reflections in Mirrors

The Hellenic folding mirrors, ornamented with relief work, and their Tuscan imitations are far fewer in number than those round hand-mirrors with handles, or tongues for handles, which came into fashion in Etruria itself towards the end of the sixth century B.C. The backs of the highly polished bronze discs are decorated with engraved pictures. A marked predilection for subjects taken from Greek mythology and a comprehensive knowledge of Greek poetry are evident. Though some examples are admittedly coarse or commonplace, there are many pieces of exquisite beauty, particularly among those dating from the fifth and fourth centuries B.C.

The owner of a mirror has the power to behold himself, can therefore 'arrange himself' as it were, and learn how to present himself as he would like to appear. One has only to mention Rembrandt's self-portraits or the ancient legend of Narcissus to realize what a fascination emanates from the reflected image of one's self. The Etruscan mirrors of known provenance all come from tombs and the precincts of tombs. This fact, together with the knowledge we have acquired of the role of mirrors in ancient times in myths and in the cults of mysteries, points to a significance extending far beyond cosmetic needs.[1] The reflected image, like the shadow, of a human being seemed to men of ancient times capable of presenting the soul as a figure with 'all the attributes of the body except the one crucial one of tangibility.' The mirror became the magic instrument by means of which a personality was created and a soul could be conjured up.

[1]The attribution of Etruscan mirrors to their correct place in the history of art and the study of the subjects depicted on them have occupied so much attention that much less has been paid to the problem of their actual significance in Etruscology.

In the Egyptian and Hittite languages, there was a close etymological connexion between the word for mirror and the word for life. Among mankind throughout the world a fear of reflections—in water or in shining discs—and of their power to cast a spell over the soul used to be common; in ancient popular customs we find many and various precautionary measures designed to shield an embryonic life, an unborn or newly born child and its mother, from mirrors. In a house where someone is dying the mirrors are screened so that the soul may not be trapped by them. It is a familiar burial practice in many countries to place a mirror in the grave with the dead. All this entitles us to assume that similar ideas lie behind the Etruscan mirrors of the dead and to believe that they served not only the normal practical purposes in life but were regarded also as a means of access and a bridge to other worlds and a vehicle for the transport of souls.

Probably one of the largest and finest Etruscan mirrors is the so-called Athrpa mirror (Fig. 3)[1] found in Perugia. It dates from about 320 B.C. Let us now look more closely at it. It is over twelve inches in length and the reflecting surface is almost eight inches in diameter. The tongue of the handle, cast in one with the mirror, would have been enclosed in a haft of turned bone or wood, as are some others which have been preserved whole.

On the reverse side of the golden-coloured bronze disc a picture is engraved. It depicts the naked bodies of young people of both sexes drawn with smooth, even-flowing, beautiful lines, against a background of folds of rich curtains, swaying like reeds, drawn just as the Greek masters of the end of the fourth century B.C. used to teach their pupils to see and represent them. Atmosphere rather than action fills the frame and the actual lines of the drawing are more significant than the objects they represent. The young winged woman in the middle, holds a hammer with which she is preparing to drive a nail into the wall above, yet even the motion of raising her arm does not appear to be an action.

No less an authority than Sir John Beazley has remarked that this style of composition in which faces portrayed side by side look out at the beholder is part of the evolution from the decoration of the East pediment of the temple of Zeus at Olympia *via* the art of Byzantium

[1]Bartholdy Collection, Berlin, Antiquarium (Fr. 146) at present in the *Kunst-gutlager* (Art-Store) at Wiesbaden.

Fig. 3. The Athrpa Mirror, approx. 320 B.C., diameter 7¾ in.

to the altar pictures of the Middle Ages. In these last, serene saints stand side by side, radiating solemnity and divinity, yet once the beholder has discovered through tradition, or through accompanying symbols such as a wheel or a tower, or through inscriptions, who each one is, he is led into a storied world of lives of saints and of miracles. Similarly, once names are put to the couples and the central figure on this mirror, wider spheres are immediately evoked for those who look at it.

Etruscan ladies of rank, like their husbands, were literate: numerous inscriptions on mirrors and jewel cases are evidence of this. They were so familiar with both Greek and Etruscan myths that all they needed to recall the tales was the names of the characters.

The Finiteness of Life

The right-hand couple, armed with spears, are, according to the inscriptions, Atlenta and Meliacr (Atalanta and Meleager). These two met in Aetolia during the famous Calydonian boar-hunt. The mirror portrays the huntress, completely naked but for elegant sandals and gorgeous necklace, as a beautiful woman rather than as a warrior maiden, but on the occasion of the hunt, mounted on horseback, she severely wounded the furious monster hiding in a thicket. Young Meleager, however, who as King of Calydon had called on all renowned warriors of Greece to join this chase, dealt it a death blow.

The successful hunter, falling head over heels in love, presented to Atalanta the hide of the boar which had been awarded as victor's prize to him. This gave rise to ill-will and quarrels and Meleager slew two of his nearest relatives, his mother's brothers, when they had taken his gift away from Atalanta. In the ensuing war he himself lost his life. Atropos, the inexorable goddess of destiny, had, when he was newly born, seized a wooden log from the fire which was burning on the hearth and entrusting it to his mother for safe-keeping had granted him breath for only so long as it remained unburned. Enraged at the slaying of her brothers, his mother flung the wood back into the blazing fire and as it fell to ashes the life of her son ebbed away.

The remains of the inscription by the head of the female figure leaning towards the youth seated opposite to Atalanta and laying her arm on his shoulder indicate that she is the goddess Turan, who corresponds to the Greek Aphrodite. Numerous illustrations prove with what enthusiasm Etruscan women had taken to their hearts the myth of the great goddess's tragic love for the handsome Adonis (or Atune as they called him in their language) which had reached them from the East *via* Hellas. Indeed the Adonis cult seems to have taken particularly firm root in Hellenistic Italy as a woman's cult.

When Persephone, goddess of the underworld, and Aphrodite quarrelled for possession of the young man, radiant in all his splendid beauty, Zeus decreed that he should belong only partly to each. Year after year Adonis dies, slain according to inexorable law by the tusks of a boar sent by Ares or Artemis to attack him; year after year the anemones are stained red by his blood, and the goddess of Love suffers the agony of parting. Lamented by Aphrodite and by all women, the youth is drawn irresistibly through the air and over the sea till he disappears into the other world.

The Nail of Fate

As though to draw attention to and illustrate the connecting link between the two couples the head of a boar is inserted at the top edge of the mirror, beside the head of Meleacr, for whom, as for his opposite number Atune, it spelt disaster. But a peculiarly Etruscan character is given to the picture by the emphasis on the power of fate to govern the lives of those depicted. For the winged female figure in the middle holding a hammer and a nail is the goddess of Fate herself. She who played such a predominant part in the faith and philosophy of the Etruscans appears here under the name Athrpa which echoes the name of the Greek Atropos, the inexorable. In Etruria the ceremonial driving in of a nail symbolized the acceptance of the inevitability of divine fate, which was believed to govern all events, both great and small. Horace makes Necessitas, companion of the Etruscan Fortuna of Praeneste,[1] carry wood-nails and bronze axe-heads in her hands. In the temple of Nortia, the Fortuna of Volsinii, the years used to be recorded by the 'year-nails' driven ceremoniously into the wall of the *cella*[2] in the shrine at the close of each year.

The parallel between the life-force and flame, and the close connexion between the hearth and procreation; the tragic view of the finiteness of life and love, and the subjection of gods and men alike

[1]Palestrina (translator's note).

[2]*Cella*—the tripartite sanctuary in an Etruscan temple which housed the images of the gods (translator's note).

to omnipotent fate; the postponement of that which is ordained by establishing a contact between the divine Moira and the mortal mother of the person doomed to die—all these are features of the Greek world of tradition which would certainly move Etruscans when they looked at such pictures as that on the Athrpa mirror. For it is obvious that from some date we have not yet been able to ascertain, their own attitude to life was determined by just such representations as this. The couples depicted here and the style of the drawing and composition are Greek, but the Etruscan atmosphere is created by the choice and by the juxtaposition of these very couples—Atalanta-Meleager and Aphrodite-Adonis—beneath the sign of the boar's head and by their being grouped around Athrpa, standing ready to hammer home her nails.

3. THE ETRUSCANS' METHOD OF RECKONING TIME AND THEIR FATALISM

The Doctrine of the Saecula[1]

One can obtain a clearer grasp of the Etruscans' distinctive religious belief in fate by studying their peculiar method of reckoning time. This is one of the principal surviving features of the once celebrated *Disciplina Etrusca* which must be regarded as being of vital significance for any understanding of the spiritual influences which actuated these people. Unfortunately what has come down to us on the subject of Etruscan conceptions of time is so fragmentary, dates from such a late period and is so confused, indeed often contradictory, that many essential features must remain obscure unless new sources of information are discovered. Moreover in examining what can be learned about the *Disciplina* from Greek and Roman philosophers, poets and grammarians, from historians and the Early Fathers, one must always consider how far what they wrote may be the product of that syncretism which affects the whole of the Hellenistic and late-ancient period and from which Etruria could not escape. An additional complication in understanding the method of reckoning time is the fact that in the relevant writings on the subject Etruscan and Roman dates appear to have become relatively soon intermingled. However, a few basic facts are known with certainty.

The Etruscans believed that different peoples each had an existence of a predetermined duration, with a beginning and an end in between

[1]*Saeculum*—age, era, century, period (translator's note).

which they grew, flourished and faded away, just as the different ages of man are all steps on his road to death. The *Nomen Etruscum* was supposed to have been assigned eight, or according to other traditions, ten *saecula* and it is a strange fact that Etruscanism as an entity in culture and history actually did begin to disappear from sight and to merge into the Roman Empire in the years in which its destiny was, according to this doctrine, fulfilled.

The notion of time expressed in the doctrine of the *saecula* indicates a tendency in the same direction as the unique preoccupation with everything connected with death and burial, of which the tombs and funerary structures speak. The Etruscans, unlike the Roman emperors from Augustus on, did not celebrate the beginning of a new era, but the end of a year, or of a *saeculum*. We must remember that in the Adonis-cult likewise attention was directed not so much to the annual return of the handsome youth and his reunion with Aphrodite as to the sorrowful parting which had to take place in accordance with immutable law.

According to the 'doctrine' a *saeculum* lasted from the end of the preceding one till the death of the last of all those who had been alive at its beginning. The length of a *saeculum* could not therefore be determined by calculation. The signs given by the gods had to be observed and their meaning understood. Everything unusual—thunderbolts and hailstorms, a plague of mice, earthquakes, an epidemic or the birth of a freak—might be a significant indication of something. Observation and interpretation then developed into a special art, the so-called *haruspicina*,[1] whose practitioners based their utterances mainly on the observation of lightning and the ritual examination of the livers of sacrificed animals.

'And so it is written that the first four *saecula* each lasted 100 years, the fifth 123, and the sixth 119, the seventh the same and the records were set down in the course of the eighth. A ninth and a tenth were still to run and when these had expired the end of the "Etruscan Name" would have come.' Thus wrote Censorinus in his *De die natali* in the beginning of the third century of the Christian era. He relied for his information on the details which the grammarian Varro gave of the

---

[1] *Haruspicina*—haruspicy (the practice) or haruspication (the function) of the *haruspex*, i.e. soothsayer or diviner, who foretells the future from the inspection of the entrails of animals offered for sacrifice (translator's note).

Tuscae historiae. From Plutarch's 'Life of Sulla' we learn that 88 B.C. was the last year of the eighth *saeculum*, mentioned above as being still in its course.

We shall discuss later the arrangement of the timing of the first four *saecula*. But the irregular numerical values given for the length of the fifth, sixth and seventh *saecula* demonstrate the important fact that the Etruscans perceived and measured time in a manner different from that which mankind to-day has come to regard as natural. The passing of time is thus measured by other than worldly events and the method of reckoning it is subject to other conceptions than those of providing guiding lines of practical usefulness in administration and in daily life. Such events as the rise or fall of a city, the victory or defeat of armies, social changes of radical effect, were thought less significant than striking natural phenomena which were considered to be signs made by celestial beings.

Destiny and the Postponement of Fate

The Etruscans worshipped *Fortuna* under many names. They believed that some secret nameless power ruled over even the greatest gods and spoke nervously of it as of a thing veiled in mystery. Unparalleled ruthlessness was considered to be one of its special characteristics. In a way which we can scarcely comprehend to-day the Etruscans felt that they were drawn into and carried away by a stream controlled from on high by these incalculable powers of destiny, against which it was useless for the individual will to struggle. Obviously this attitude made the writing of history in the sense in which we understand it impossible. The skilled *haruspex* who can recognize and interpret the will of the gods plays a more decisive role than the politician or the general who merely fulfils what has been ordained by fate.

In a world thus based on subjection to the will of the gods, however, one thing still remains within the power of the individual man, namely the possibility of getting into communication with the gods through prayers, sacrifices and expiation ceremonies. He who does so may, by performing these rites, arrive at such a degree of certainty and perfection that some deferment may be granted to him, though not indeed any absolute reprieve. Thus once again it becomes plain why the priest is the central figure of Etruscan life and why all the high offices in Etruria are priestly.

An individual's fate can be postponed by ten years, all Etruria's by so much as thirty. This theory of postponement of fate made it possible to explain individual cases and allowed for reconciliation between what ought to happen according to the observed portents, and what could be seen actually to happen.

This tendency to take exceptions into account and to allow for them shows itself also in other expressions of the spiritual life of the Etruscans. They became the creators of an art of portraiture based on the uniqueness and the individuality of the person portrayed, which elude standardization.

In the doctrine of the *saecula* itself we can trace the same attitude to life which produced a belief in the possibility of postponement of destiny being granted subject to certain conditions. In the form in which it has reached us this doctrine attempts to explain why a period of history may go on and last longer even when according to the astrologers and soothsayers it ought already to have come to an end.

The Metal Ages

One obvious result of this way of thinking was the theory of the perpetually deteriorating metal ages, common all over the world. The silver age follows the gold and in its turn is replaced by the copper age, just as the lucky shepherd of the fairy tale climbs the tree which bears on its lowest boughs the copper city, a day's travel further up the silver city, and finally at the top in the crowning golden branches the wondrously beautiful princess in the golden castle. In the realm of history we come across this same tale, but it is enriched by a fourth era—the iron age, which corresponds to the harsh present day—regarded at any given epoch as unfriendly and ruthless. This more recent conception, possible only after iron had become cheap i.e. since approximately the eighth century B.C., seems to have spread no less widely than the older theory based on three phases. In Etruscan terms these four phases correspond to the first four *saecula* which the simplified estimation of time renders as each lasting one hundred years.

The earliest description of this theory concerning the ages of the world which has been preserved is to be found painted with broad strokes in the epic of the Greek poet Hesiod known as 'Works and Days', Ἔργα καὶ ἡμέραι: 'The first race of speaking men which the immortal gods, who dwell on Olympus, created was golden . . . and they lived their lives like gods without griefs, remote from trouble and sorrow, and miserable old age did not come near them, . . . while the Earth of its own volition constantly bestowed nourishing fruits on them. . . .' Later however the gods created 'still another race, a much inferior one of silver, which could not be compared with the golden one in body or in spirit.' 'And now Cronos created another, a third race of speaking men, a brazen race, which in no way resembled the silver race, but which sprang from ashtrees and was savage and frightful . . . All their weapons were of bronze and their houses were bronze, the implements for tilling the land too; at that time there was not yet any black iron . . . Terrible though they were, black death seized them, and they departed from the radiant light of the sun.' The poet now breaks boldly away from the tradition of the myth and the natural sequence and lets this race of bronze men be followed by the splendid race of Homeric heroes whom he glorifies as demi-gods. Lastly they are followed by the awful race of the present, the iron men. 'Would that I were not myself one of these men of the fifth age— would that I had died before, or had been born later.' However, 'Zeus will destroy this race of speaking men too when they are born with greying temples.' Shame and just retribution 'hasten away from men to join the family of the gods . . . all that remains is sorrow and misery among mortal rulers. There is naught which avails against evil.'

The nucleus of the three-phase tradition can easily be recognized in this version by Hesiod, for here the last, the Iron Age, is basically but a repetition of what has already been said about the Bronze Age and contains nothing essentially new. Finally the insertion of the race of heroes between the third and what would have been the fourth but now becomes the fifth stage, i.e. the era of mankind, reveals the existence of a conflict between mythical chronology and historical experience of the situation around 700 B.C. when the epic was composed. The poet finds a way out by recasting the myth.[1] In Hellas this process was further developed by the retreat of mythical notions as such before the practical method of reckoning which then asserted

---

[1] In much the same way, Solon, one hundred years later, explained the similar contradiction with which he himself was faced in that he remained hale and hearty after his seventieth year, contrary to his own theory on the subject: '. . . erase that, and resent it not that my thoughts were more rational than thine. Alter thy words, Oh sweet poet, and sing thus to me: "May death deal me the fatal blow in my eightieth year!"'.

itself, freed from all teleological[1] accessories, and which was based on the celebration every four years of the Olympiads.

The Etruscans at some date which cannot be precisely determined also came to use as a means of reckoning time the nails which were driven into the temple of Nortia during the ceremonies at the close of each year. It is also possible that individual cities each had their own method of reckoning like Rome's *ab urbe condita*—'from the founding of the city'. Nonetheless they remained conscious of time as established by the *saecula* doctrine, which grouped the years as they passed into periods of time defined for ever by a decision of the gods.

'World-Week' and 'World-Year'

It has not been possible yet to make out just when this theory, with its extension to a total of eight phases, acquired its prophetic character, pointing beyond the present to a predestined end. The use of dates certainly appears to be a later phenomenon, for if one reckons back from the final date of 88 B.C. which has been handed down to us, using the figures given, viz. 119, 119 and 123 years, and for the sake of argument assumes that the *saeculum* then ending was like its two predecessors also 119 years long, one arrives only at 568 B.C. Perhaps the Nortia nails did go back as far as that, but we do not seem to have gained anything definite from this evidence. If we then add the four periods each of one hundred years to the calculated 568 B.C.—which it must be admitted can be regarded as only approximate—we arrive at 968 B.C. as the year in which Etruscan time actually began. This then, if we are to regard it as having any validity at all as a historical fact, would mean that the Etruscans ascribed their own beginnings to an earlier date than those of Rome, which incidentally corresponds to the Roman view. But this does not help us to decide whether they had any knowledge of the early iron civilization which was beginning about that time to flourish in central Italy and which is known to us as the Villanova culture, from the name of a place in the environs of Bologna, and it seems doubtful whether they did.

The decisive event, an intellectual achievement going far beyond Hesiod, was the evolution of an eight-part time structure out of the myth of the perpetually deteriorating metal ages by doubling the number of those ages. That is to say there emerged the idea of a

[1]Teleology—the doctrine of the final causes of things (translator's note).

'world-week', at the end of which a new 'week' would begin, granted to a new race of men, and possibly under the rule of new gods. At the end of every week, i.e. on the ninth day, the Etruscans were in the habit of paying their respects to their kings and consulting them, according to the evidence of Macrobius. Although there is a suspicion here of late Babylonian influences at work, later vague accounts of a 'Great Year', supposed to be an Etruscan conception, at the end of which everything would have returned to its own place, do seem to have some meaning when examined against this background.

Gods Who Wield Thunderbolts; and the End of Time

These conclusions, based on rather scanty data, gain more colour and background from certain features of Etruscan mythology. For according to tradition the Etruscans acknowledged a league of eight powerful divinities, all capable of throwing thunderbolts, at whose head stood the ninth, the leader Tinia himself, the mighty Lord of Heaven, whom the Romans equated with Jupiter on account of his status and power. Members of the group were the goddesses Menrva (Minerva, Athena), Turan (Venus, Aphrodite) and Uni (Juno, Hera) and the gods Sethlans (Vulcan, Hephaistos), Satres (Saturnus) and Mari (Mars, Ares). The names of the other two have not been handed down. Each of these gods was supposed to have his own sort of lightning, recognizable by its distinctive colour, and his own fixed domain in heaven from which he hurled down his thunderbolts. But Tinia held three glittering red thunderbolts. The first he threw at his own discretion, to indicate assent or dissent, as the case might be. The second, which could bring about good but at the same time caused harm, he could throw only if all the twelve great gods (including those which did not wield thunderbolts) had previously given their consent. In the organized hierarchy of the gods these formed the Council of Twelve at whose head was Tinia again—the *Di Consentes*, the Romans called them. But before throwing the third and most fearful of all the thunderbolts Tinia must first consult the mightiest powers of destiny, the shrouded divinities themselves; for this thunderbolt annihilated what it struck and radically changed everything, both for individuals and for all mankind.

It is related of the *Di Consentes* that they were called 'the co-existing gods' 'because they come into existence together and together they perish' and for the same reason and because they are twelve in number they have also been described as the gods of the Zodiac. This simultaneous destruction, linked with the ending of the 'world-week' in a holocaust caused by lightning on the ninth 'world-day', seems to indicate, as in the Edda, the end of a generation of gods, in this case the gods grouped round Tinia, just as in Greek mythology the reign of Cronos was followed by that of Zeus.

A certain confusion and vagueness about the *saecula* doctrine was inevitable at the time when according to its prophecies the end of the *Nomen Etruscum* was due yet life had not been extinguished in a catastrophe. But here too the *Disciplina* provided a way out. The explanation given was that in the existence of a whole people as in the life of a single human being each phase of development contained its own potentialities, limitations and dangers. As man grew older and his faculties diminished he also lost the capacity of understanding the signs of the gods and he resembled a runner in a race, or a four-in-hand, running aimlessly outside the marked track. Moreover a prediction attributed to a nymph Vegoia (of whom we know nothing further) foretold that in the penultimate *saeculum* men would, out of covetousness, use cunning and deception to damage, destroy and remove from their places the boundary stones which had been erected to mark the limits for them. From this pronouncement we can also draw the inference that the *saecula* doctrine had preserved the notion, originally conceived in the early Iron Age, and expressed in the Metal Ages' theory, that conditions would deteriorate steadily until ultimately everything was destroyed.

The original conception of time on an eight-phase basis seems to have been ultimately extended, along the lines of the theory of postponement of destiny, to the idea of a ten-phase system. What led to this appears to have been the obscurity of the whole situation together with the well-known delight of later Hellenism in philosophical speculation, in learned combinations of elements essentially quite different, and in rational interpretation of religious hypotheses. 'The wisest of the Etrurians' had indeed announced that according to the signs of the gods the year 88 B.C. was the beginning of the end. Yet only forty-four years later, after Caesar's murder and when the appearance of a comet was terrifying the populace, the Etruscan seer Vulcatius announced in the presence of a Roman public gathering the

Plate III.   Detail from the Tomba degli Auguri at Tarquinii

(Photo: Walter Dräyer)

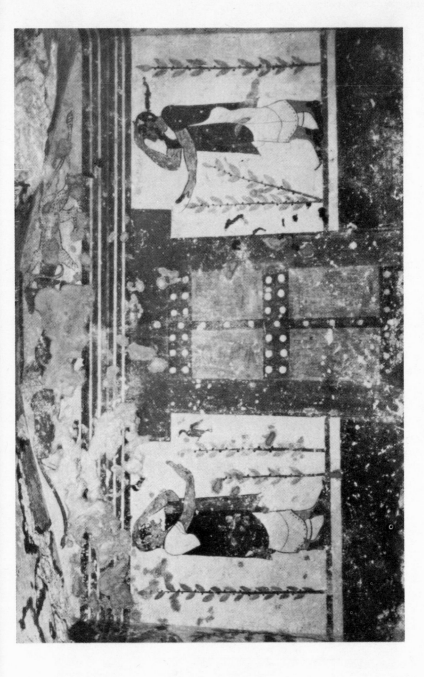

Plate IV.   Detail from the Tomba degli Auguri at Tarquinii

(Photo: Walter Dräyer)

end of the ninth *saeculum* which he at the same time described as 'the penultimate'.

4. SANCTIFICATION OF SPACE

The Principle of Quartering

As is generally the case when men's conduct is guided more by supernatural occurrences than by worldly experience, space and time are conceived in the *Disciplina Etrusca* as being both subject to the same rules. The doctrine originally conceived of time as passing through four steadily deteriorating eras, and heaven and earth were regarded as being quartered by two immense invisible intersecting axes.

In the north at the summit Tinia sits enthroned. He looks towards the south, dividing the world by his glance into an eastern and a western half. The part on his left, out of which the constellations rise, is regarded as propitious, that on his right is the calamitous side. For a suppliant of Tinia's, facing him, the different halves have of course the reverse significance. In everyday speech therefore right and left have the opposite meaning from that in astrology and in divine worship. The power of good or bad fortune in the four quarters varies according to the proximity or remoteness of Tinia, so space is bisected a second time by a lateral axis having its two extremities in the regions of the rising and the setting sun. The north-east quarter is considered to be favourable in every respect, the north-west is the most unfavourable, the south-east less favourable, the south-west less unfavourable. If one were to transfer the names of the different metals of the world-ages to these four quarters then gold would go to the north-east, silver to the south-east, copper or copper-bronze to the south-west and black iron to the north-west, where dwells the evil Anti-Tinia, Veiovis as the Romans called him.

Further regular sectionalizing of the quarters created firstly eighths and ultimately sixteenths, which was particularly convenient for ever more meticulous observation of lightning, omens and bird-flight, but was also expedient for priestly appraisal of the livers of sacrificed animals. For these livers were treated as though they were a reflection so to speak of the vault of heaven and its divisions and interpreted accordingly. The bronze image of such a liver was found last century near Piacenza and was probably used in its day as a model for instruction in the art of *haruspicina*. It is divided on its upper surface into no

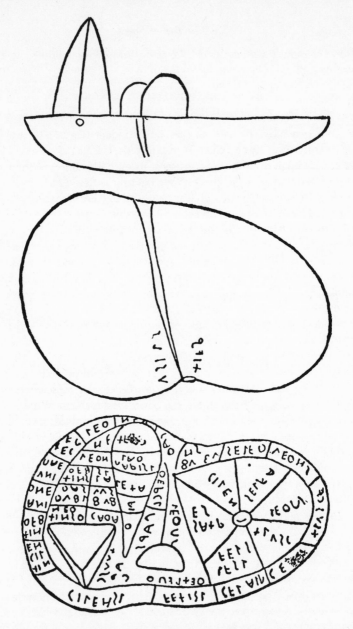

Fig. 4. The bronze liver of Piacenza: (*a*) side-view; (*b*) from below, showing the line of orientation from north to south; (*c*) seen from above

fewer than forty sections, each with the name of a divinity inscribed on it. Martianus Capella, in his work *De Nuptiis Philologiae et Mercurii* —'On the Marriage of Philology and Mercury'—written in the second half of the fifth century of the Christian era, describes just such a complicated celestial system. Taken together these two pieces of evidence are some proof of the ultimate evolution of the initially simple system into such hair-splitting refinements, but though important in themselves they can give us little certainty about the original form of the concept.

We may assume that the nine lightning gods, each of whom was supposed to have his own abode, his own permanent portion of the heaven, were distributed evenly around the edge of the circle in the eight sections evolved from the four quarters of the whole. For the ninth, the paramount Lord of Heaven and all its Regions, the place reserved is then not the geographical north, but the magnetic north, indicated by the Pole Star. Throughout Europe and Asia we find the Pole Star playing an important role in countless myths and sagas, sometimes with just such a meaning, sometimes as top of the tree of the world.

Laying a City's Foundation According to Religious Laws

This method of dividing space is indeed a prerequisite for observing and understanding the signs given by the gods who determine the division of time in the world and is thus in general the basis of the Etruscan notion of time. In addition, however, it determines the feeling of belonging to a place for the individual and for the population as a whole, by establishing boundaries and elucidating religious references. A town laid out in accordance with such principles *'rite'* i.e. correctly from a religious point of view, is not primarily a place for enclosing a group of dwellings and businesses, but the consecrated centre of a world controlled and maintained by the gods.

The Romans held that it was essential when laying foundations or planning a city to be skilled in and to employ the rules evolved by the Etruscans. The legendary heart of the metropolis on the Tiber, the *urbs quadrata*, 'quartered city', on the Palatine Hill was reputed to have been laid-out in the prescribed Tuscan style. Roman camps too, with their four gates and their streets intersecting at right-angles, revealed the influence of related if not identical notions.

Plutarch reports that when Romulus founded his city he had 'men come from Tuscany who prescribed all the details in accordance with certain sacred ordinances and writings, and taught them to him as in a religious rite. A circular trench was dug around what is now the Comitium, and in this were deposited first-fruits of all things, the use of which was sanctioned by custom as good and by nature as necessary; and finally, every man brought a small portion of the soil of his native land and these were cast in among the first-fruits and mingled with them. They call this trench, as they do the heavens, by the name of "*mundus*". Then taking this as a centre, they marked out the city in a circle round it. And the founder, having shod a plough with a brazen ploughshare, and having yoked to it a bull and a cow, himself drove a deep furrow round the boundary lines, while those who followed after him had to turn the clods, which the plough threw up, inwards towards the city, and suffer no clod to lie turned outwards. With this line they mark out the course of the wall . . . And where they purposed to put in a gate, there they took the share out of the ground, lifted the plough over, and left a vacant space. And this is the reason why they regard all the wall as sacred except the gates; but if they held the gates sacred, it would not be possible, without religious scruples, to bring into and send out of the city things which are necessary, and yet unclean.'[1]

Notes found here and there in late classical works reveal how the ceremonies described here were worked out in meticulous detail, how the clothing had to be worn in a certain way, the plough had to go counter-clockwise, the cow (white as prescribed) had to be led from the inside while the bull (white also) was led from the outside. Most important of all, however, is the revelation that on the occasion when the location of the *mundus* was fixed and the city's boundaries traced out, the main street intersection with its four equal arms branching out, which determined the layout of the centre of the future city, was also marked out, the *cardo* running from north to south and the *decumanus*, which is the east-west axis, crossing it at its central point. The *mundus* situated at the point of intersection of the two then turns out to be a shaft leading directly into the underworld. The great stone which sealed it was called in Rome the *lapis manalis*—'stone of souls'—and when it was lifted up three times a year on the days dedicated to the divinities of the underworld the *manes*, i.e. the spirits of the dead, rose out of the

[1]Translation by Bernadotte Perrin.

mundus. The gateway of the mournful gods of the underworld was opened, as they put it.

The reader who would gain an understanding of the conception of life held by the human beings who lived in such a town must visualize it to himself. He must picture a city laid out in this way, its overall plan being determined as it were by the design of its foundation and by the cults being regularly practised there. The city, built in accordance with the sacred rules, *more Etrusco*, rose on rocks of tuff which fell steeply away on all sides, cut off from the world outside by the water flowing in the surrounding *fossi.* The centre was indicated by a shaft leading to the underworld, which served at the appointed times as a way of ascent for souls and spirits and which received the offerings of the harvests, or sacrifices. But beyond the streams lay the broad ring of graves, which could not fail to be seen from the dwellings of the living. These were especially conspicuous in the rock-tomb cemeteries with their high façades carved out of the cliffs, on the plain above which the tops of the mounds of the dead, pressed close to one another, rose and fell like an undulating line of waves.

The Consecrated City

A city of this type was a sacred entity, a piece of architecture exalted far above the ordinary purposes of a mere place to live in: it was a cosmic creation in which was manifest the order of the universe, for all to behold. The inhabitants of such a city lived surrounded by the dead, and grouped themselves round the gate to the underworld. The plan of their houses, streets and gates assigned them their position within the quarters of the heavens, which Tinia himself and the gods who have power over lightning and over time had determined. So they lived in the present, but their life was surrounded by thoughts of the Beyond. We can gain some conception of their way of looking at life from accounts which describe how the people of such towns, at their head priests wearing the masks of the demons of the underworld, would burst forth from the walls of their cities like armies of the dead, ferocious, hurling flames and serpents against besieging enemies.

How could such a form of existence have been tolerated in the ancient world if death were seen as an actual end and the destruction of the *Nomen Etruscum* as the dawn of nothingness? The profusion of pictures and gifts in the burial chambers teaches us clearly enough that the Etruscans believed in an enhanced life after death. To illustrate this they used the pomp and colour with which they sought to intensify their own existence and which made their enjoyment of life more keen. Then again they held beliefs according to which the dead could be turned into immortal gods through offerings of the blood of specified animals and certain sacrificial actions. On the front of their rock-tombs and on the tombstones modelled on them they depicted a gate as a symbol, proof of their belief that dying and walking from one room to another represented comparable experiences.

It remains uncertain whether any ideas of purification or any ethical challenges were contained in their doctrine that a predestined deterioration of the world was taking place in obedience to some law. As is usual in secret cults and mystery religions the heart of the matter lies largely in the dark and can scarcely be grasped by people whose thought processes are different and who live another way of life.

CHAPTER II

Elements of Spiritual Unity

I. TRADITIONAL ACCOUNTS OF THE ORIGIN OF THE ETRUSCANS

The Art of Portraiture as Evidence

THE Etruscans obviously acquired at an early date a capacity to discriminate between general tendencies and individual features in matters governed by Nature, Fate and Chance,[1] which made them masters of the art of portraiture. Their contribution to European representational art is a permanent and substantial one and the accomplishment with which they created portrait-busts and heads excels that of Rome in this field. Even the figures on the later sarcophagi and urns, often somewhat hastily and stylistically modelled, reveal this eye for personality and for physiognomy. Even when they are not really works of art—as for instance those on most of the countless urn-lids of terracotta or stone to be seen in the museums of Perugia, Chiusi and Volterra—they do give such a lively portrait that people were ready and willing to recognize themselves in them.

Such is the variety of heads and faces, the individuality and liveliness of their expression, that the most uninformed observer cannot fail to be moved by them. Frequently indeed realism is carried to the absolute limit of probability.

For example there is the fat bloated man with the plump fleshy bald head and broad short nose above the small thick-lipped mouth—exactly what we have always imagined a typical Etruscan would look

[1]'Man's life is bounded by three powers: by nature, to whom not more than 120 years are granted; by fate or destiny, to which 90 years, i.e. three revolutions of Saturn, bring destruction unless perhaps the favour of other constellations may yet prevail over his third revolution; and finally by fortune, i.e. chance, to which can be attributed everything which comes from outside such as revolution, fire and the effects of poison,' says Servius with reference to the doctrine of the Etruscans.

27

like, because of Catullus' casual description of the *obesus Etruscus*—'the corpulent Etruscan'. Yet nearby, in the same museum in Chiusi, there crops up the clear-cut skull of a man of priestly calling: we can tell his profession not only by the great ring on the ring finger of his left hand and the alms bowl in his right, but also by the close-fitting cowl knotted under his chin. This face, with its regular features, has a distinct look of the Roman and its broad round chin, firm cheeks and small energetic mouth speak of self-discipline and will-power.

Then we see the face of a man, apparently elderly, with high and noble brow, short projecting chin, sharp high cheekbones above hollow cheeks, and large ears. The tightly pursed mouth lies almost in a straight line beneath the powerful straight nose.[1]

Fig. 5. Sections of a tomb painting, end of the sixth century B.C.

A tale of toil and trouble is told in the coarse-boned face of a dead man portrayed on the lid of a Volterra terracotta urn[2] reclining side by side with his elderly wife, who is looking at him. These figures are modelled in the superficial impressionist style of the late period and the fact that the skull is disproportionately large in comparison with the body gives the figure an earthy realism not easily forgotten. The short fleshy nose projects above the powerful mouth and deep lines are drawn from the nose to the corners of the mouth. The round face with eyes

[1]Second half of third century, B.C., *Museo Civico*, Chiusi.
[2]In the *Museo Guarnacci*, Volterra.

gazing into the distance, a firm chin and a furrowed brow beneath bristling hair, is framed by sticking-out ears.

And how varied were the women! The more one studies their faces and compares their figures as one wanders through the halls and galleries of the museums, the more impressed one is by the multiplicity of types these people exhibit. Yet there is not a feature to be seen which does not fit into the picture of the European. Any attempt to classify them into types fails and no one can be satisfied with the suggestion that this variety reveals a process of disintegration in Etruria during the last centuries before Christ.

Indeed much of what we learn from such sources as are preserved of the earlier history of the Etruscans commends acceptance of this very diversity as characteristic of them. As far back as we can see into the past they seem never to have been a nation homogeneous in blood or type and as far forward as we can follow their history they seem never to have developed completely into one.

The Legend of the Original Home in Lydia

Herodotus gives an account of the origin of the Etruscans which sounds like a fairy tale. He says that this goes back to Lydian sources. According to this story they actually came from Lydia, that prehistoric kingdom in north-west Asia Minor whose capital was Sardis, and which has become celebrated through the stories of Gyges and his ring and of King Croesus. Herodotus says that in his day the Lydians told the following tale of the Tyrrhenian migration:

'When Atys, son of Manes, was king, a terrible famine afflicted the whole land of Lydia. For some time the Lydians bore it patiently, but when it showed no signs of coming to an end, they began to look around for remedies. One thought of one thing, another had another idea and that is how dice-games, games with bones, ball-games and all sorts of other games were invented, but not board-games which the Lydians do not claim to have invented. The plan they adopted to counter their feelings of hunger was the following: one whole day they played games so that they did not crave for food at all and the next day they ate and did not play at all. In this manner they whiled away eighteen years. As, however, the affliction grew no less but indeed rather grew worse, the King of the Lydians divided them all into two groups and made them draw lots, who should stay and who should emigrate. And the King joined those who were to remain; but to those who had to leave the country he gave his son, whose name was Tyrrhenus. Those whose lot was to depart then went down to Smyrna and built themselves vessels in which to travel. They then loaded on to these all the equipment which they might need and sailed away to look for somewhere to make a home and a living. At length, after sailing past the lands of many peoples they came to the land of the Umbricans and in that place they built themselves cities and there they live to this very day. And they changed their name from Lydians to a name they took from that of their King's son who had led them hither and called themselves Tyrrhenians.'

The 'Umbricans' mentioned here are the Umbrians, of whom it is also said elsewhere that they originally held the whole of Central Italy. But King Atys, during whose reign the migration is supposed to have taken place, belonged to the old Lydian dynasty which, according to the testimony of this same Herodotus, gave way in the second half of the thirteenth century B.C. to the descendants of Hercules and Omphale, the so-called Heraclidae. This would make the date the Etruscans landed on the coast of Central Italy 300 years earlier than the Etruscans' own theory of time fixed it. Thus it would appear to be part of the general migration of peoples which affected all the countries of the Eastern Mediterranean and which is usually known as the Aegean or Great Migration.

Genealogical Links

Another Greek account, also dating back at least as far as the fourth century B.C., makes the hero Tyrsenos (Tyrrhenus) a native of Mysia. Like Tarchon, the legendary founder of Tarquinii (who, however, judging by the name, is probably identical with him), and like Latinus and like Rhome,[1] the wife of Aeneas whose name the city of Rome is alleged to preserve, he is supposed to be a child of Telephus, who was a son of the Mysian Hercules.

This interpretation is derived, like the Lydian story of Herodotus, from similarity of names, from later identification of families with persons and from relationships between old Mediterranean languages which are no longer clear to us. Its object was to explain a situation in which Latins and Etruscans, Rome and her northern neighbours, were

[1] Or Roma (translator's note).

closely linked with each other culturally and probably also politically and were indeed, according to the findings of the experts, scarcely distinguishable from one another. Thus Hesiod, in his 'Theogony', towards the end of the eighth century B.C. calls Agrius, Latinus and Telegonus—sons of Ulysses by the sorceress Circe—'rulers over all the noble and renowned Tyrsenians, in the heart of the holy islands in the far distance' and so establishes a connexion with the 'Odyssey'.

It is well known that the Romans, for their part, traced their own origin to Homeric Troy through Aeneas and his doomed armies. This of course is approximately the same area as that from which, by the accounts quoted above, the Tyrrhenians were believed to have come. The legend of the flight of Aeneas clearly played a certain part in the Etruscan districts adjacent to Rome as early as the fifth century B.C., for votive statuettes dating from that period were recently found in Veii which show a beardless young man, armed with helmet and shield, carrying an old man on his shoulders. The style of this representation makes it certain that it is intended to portray Aeneas rescuing his old father from Troy in flames.[1]

Whatever may have been the origin of this sort of tradition it is at any rate plain that the Etruscans themselves, at least in the last centuries of their history, were familiar with these and similar genealogies and theories of origin and claimed them for the nation or at any rate for single families or groups of families.

We see from Virgil how firmly Herodotus's story took root. Virgil himself came from the northern Etruscan city of Mantua and was familiar with the ideas, customs and cults of the Etruscans. In the 'Aeneid' he refers to the Tyrrhenians as a matter of course as Lydians. Then to confirm this view from another direction we know from Tacitus that at the time of the Roman emperors the inhabitants of Sardis, the ancient royal seat, could appeal to their blood-relationship with the Tarquinians.

No doubt the Etruscans felt a need to increase their prestige and to assert themselves *vis-à-vis* Rome and were ambitious to prove a personal and national link with the heroes of the Greek epics: these feelings would promote speculations and interpretations of such a nature. It seems from the evidence of countless urn-reliefs that in those last pre-Christian centuries the Greek tales were eagerly taken up and the

[1]Rome: *Villa Giulia*. Clay: height 8 in.

Etruscans were anxious to extend their own history, which was some-what short by Italian standards, into the past of the ancient peoples of Greek Asia Minor. There is no lack of instances of this kind of thing in the history of the noble families and dynasties of Europe.

The picture which a nation forms of itself, of its natural attributes, its heritage and its ancestors, can greatly influence its conduct. The picture does not necessarily remain the same at all periods of time and of course its connexion with historical facts may be limited. Because the Etruscans, from about the fourth century B.C. onwards, believed more and more in their origin in Asia Minor, they were undoubtedly particularly receptive to religious and spiritual inspiration from that area. Much of what we read about the customs and attitudes of the Etruscans was generally recorded at a later date and ought really to be seen as having arisen out of such a context and be so evaluated, rather than being accepted (as it often is) as 'typically Lydian' or 'typically Asia Minor' and regarded as decisive in arriving at a verdict on the question of the origin of the Etruscans.

Moreover, we know that the evolution of a nation is a complicated and multiple process which, like all growth, takes place largely in the dark, and this is true of the origins of the Etruscans also. On the other hand, there is the greatly simplified story, which we find for the first time in the reign of the Emperor Augustus in the writings of Dionysius of Halicarnassus, according to which the Tyrrhenians were really nothing but a community which had been resident from earliest times in Central Italy and whose customs and habits were peculiar to them-selves; but this alternative can no longer be considered as convincing either.

It is essential to break away from the idea that the history of any nation must necessarily go back into the beginnings of time. Our conception of nationhood is recent and has a romantic basis. As its applicability to present-day conditions is by no means unquestioned, we certainly should not hasten to apply it to ancient and prehistoric conditions.

Diversity of the Population

The various Etruscan city-states reveal themselves in the centuries of which we have a more precise picture as so individual in everything they have bequeathed to us that we can speak of a homogeneous culture only with reserve. In particular any attempt to draw a line between them and their Umbrian and Latin neighbours meets with great difficulties.

Within Etruria's boundaries there is only a relatively small and limited area, the territory between Sarteano and Chiusi, in which are found the so-called *canopi* (canopic jars), i.e. cinerary urns in the form of human heads, which combine austerity of form with exuberant vitality and still make a strong appeal even to the modern observer. The boundaries between Tarquinii and Cerveteri can be traced by the distribution of the different types of tombs and burial customs. The cupola-tombs of Populonia evolved in their own manner. Every Etruscan city-state needs to be explored individually to trace the origin and nature of its inhabitants. In view of this radical diversity it is difficult to be convinced by the theory of a group of culturally superior immigrants of a master class coming by land or sea into this country and dominating a less highly evolved population already long settled there.

The people of Chiusi are also described as *Camertes Umbri* i.e. as Umbrians. In Cerveteri Greeks and Etruscans lived together and Virgil and his commentator Servius testify that the population of Mantua was in no way homogeneous. Thebans, Umbrians and Sarsines (who are also credited with having founded Perugia), Veneti, Euganeans, Ligurians and Gauls are all mentioned. The Etruscans were the leaders, it is said, but the role of the Veneti was also not insignificant. It is well known that Rome too emerged from a fusion of tribal groups with different languages.

What is much more to the point is to find out what exactly was the unifying element which so linked the Etruscans together that the Romans and also the Greeks could consider and treat them as a self-contained nation and which led them to give themselves the name of '*Rasenna*', which differed from that given to them by both Greeks and Romans.

2. ALPHABET AND LANGUAGE

Certainly the most important testimonies to Etruscan unity are their language and the alphabet in which it is transmitted to us. Since the eighteenth century research into the difficult problems posed by these subjects has been a specialized science, Etruscology in the narrower sense, whose roots in Italy lie in the Renaissance.

The Alphabet

To read the writing is not in itself difficult, since the alphabet used is of Greek extraction. We know the sound-value of each of the signs. In the cemetery of Marsigliana on the lower reaches of the Albegna a carefully carved rectangular ivory tablet was found, measuring 2 in. by $3\frac{1}{2}$ in. On its sunken inner surface were preserved remains of wax and traces of writing. An alphabet of twenty-six letters is notched from right to left into one side of the slightly raised rim framing it and evidently served as a model for the user of this dainty writing equip-

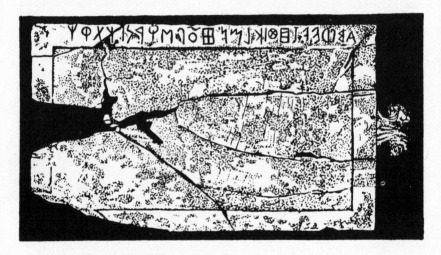

Fig. 6. Ivory writing tablet from Marsigliana d'Albegna, about 700 B.C., length $3\frac{1}{2}$ in.

ment. The tablet dates from about 700 B.C. (See Fig. 6.) Similar discoveries in Formello near Veii, Viterbo, Cerveteri and other places all support the view that the art of writing was introduced into Etruria at that time and quickly spread beyond the boundaries of the different city-states.

Nevertheless it seems somewhat strange that certain characters appear in these early lists of letters for which there existed no need in the language, while the much discussed sign for the sound F which resembled an 8 was still missing. The process of adapting the system of writing, which may have been introduced from Cumae or from its

Plate V.   Detail from a Sarcophagus at Cerveteri   (*Archives photographiques—Paris*)

Plate VI.   Reverse of bronze mirror showing Cephalos carried off by Eos

(*Vatican Museum*)

predecessor Pithecusae on Ischia,[1] to their own speech-sounds seems to have been carried out only a little later.

This adoption of the script *en bloc* is in line with the acceptance by Etruria of many other spiritual and cultural ideas from the Hellenes from the eighth century B.C. onwards. But whereas elsewhere alphabets derived from the Greek often deviated considerably in detail from one another, the Etruscans, otherwise so inclined to individualism, seem to have arrived at one single system of writing which was obviously obligatory for all.

The Language Position in Old Etruria

To form any judgment about the actual speech is however much harder, even to-day. Inscriptions give us only very slight indications of differences in dialect, but doubtless it was otherwise in the spoken language which was never recorded in writing. It is not even probable that all the diverse types of inhabitants who composed the population of the individual cities communicated with each other in Etruscan in their day to day contacts. We should rather assume that, say, the *Camertes Umbri* of Chiusi or the Sarsines of Perugia used as their colloquial language a basically Umbrian tongue, while the inhabitants of Cerveteri, to whom the Romans in olden days used to send their sons for tuition and training, talked among themselves in some dialect which bore a resemblance to Latin. People in the Etruscan city of Falerii spoke a vernacular related to Latin but also Tuscan, if we go by the evidence of inscriptions. Finally, potsherds found there with Etruscan words on them and the report of Pliny the Younger that an aged holm-oak on the Vatican hill bore an Etruscan dedicatory inscription lead us to the conclusion that there was a certain degree of multilingualism in early Rome.

[1] A. Rehm, *Hdbch. d. Arch.* 1st issue, p. 207: 'But it can well be said that from the epigraphic angle there is no valid argument which can be advanced against the derivation of the Etruscan alphabet from the Cumanian and much which can be in favour of it e.g. the outlines ⌐ and the five-stroke ∧∧ .' Pithecusae, Cumae's predecessor on Ischia, is now beginning to emerge more clearly thanks to the excavations of C. Buchner. The *skyphos* [scyphus—large drinking cup—translator's note] found there with the geometric paintings and the Nestor inscription presents for the first time in Greek a system of dots, admittedly not of the same type as that used after about 550 B.C. esp. in southern Etruria and in Etruscan Campania, but nevertheless with a separation of parts of sentences by means of double dots. The theory that the Etruscans brought a syllabic writing with them from the East is somewhat weakened as a result of this discovery.

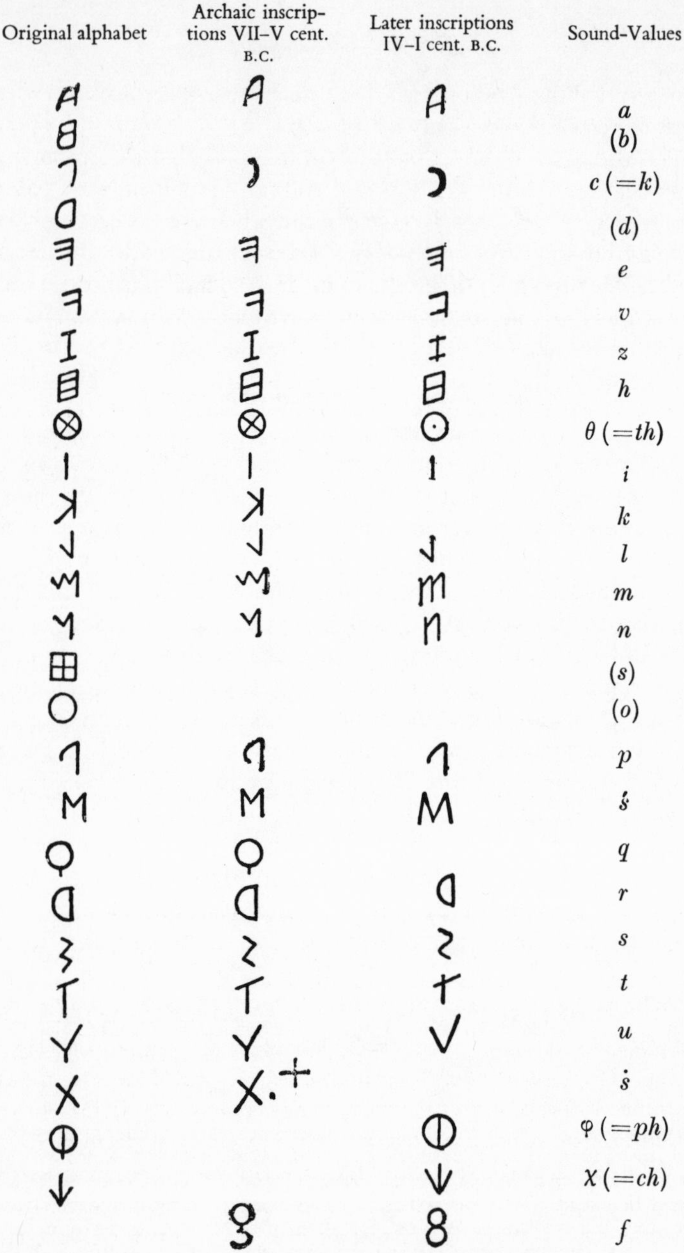

Original alphabet	Archaic inscriptions VII–V cent. B.C.	Later inscriptions IV–I cent. B.C.	Sound-Values
𝐴	𝐴	𝐴	*a*
𝐵			(*b*)
⅂	𐤂	𐤂	*c* (=*k*)
𝐷			(*d*)
𝟛	𝟛	𝟛	*e*
𝖥	𝖥	𝖥⅂	*v*
𝐈	𝐈	𝐈	*z*
𐤄	𐤄	𐤄	*h*
⊗	⊗	⊙	θ (=*th*)
I	I	ı	*i*
𝖪	𝖪		*k*
𝐿	𝐿	𝐿	*l*
𝖬	𝖬	m	*m*
𝖭	𝖭	n	*n*
⊞			(*s*)
O			(*o*)
𝖯	𝖯	𝖯	*p*
M	M	W	ś
Q	Q		*q*
𝐷	𝐷	𝐷	*r*
ξ	ξ	ξ	*s*
𝖳	𝖳	𝖸	*t*
𝖸	𝖸	𝖵	*u*
𝖷	𝖷.✝		ṡ
Φ		Φ	φ (=*ph*)
↓		↓	χ (=*ch*)
	8	8	*f*

Fig. 7. Etruscan alphabet

From Livy we learn that the language of the town-dwellers differed from that of the country people. The Etrurian tongue disappeared surprisingly quickly wherever the Romans gained a footing and this is an added reason for thinking that it was perhaps not in fact a popular vernacular. At the same time, some sound changes which occurred between the archaic and the later periods and which have led research workers to distinguish between early and late Etruscan are evidence of its being a living language and of its adaptability to the laws of history.

The language itself has hitherto defied all attempts to classify it beyond doubt as belonging exclusively to any one of the families of languages known to us. This is not so much due, as in the case of the Egyptian hieroglyphs and the cuneiform texts of Mesopotamia, to difficulty in deciphering as to the relatively small amount of words and forms which are available to us and to the fact that those deal with such a limited aspect of life.

As a well-known Etruscologist has written, it is as though someone trying to obtain a grasp of a modern language had only announcements of deaths and inscribed votive offerings at his disposal. We have names, dates, words indicating kinships, titles of offices, some verbs and a few single words recorded, not very accurately, by Roman writers, and not much more is preserved. The possibility of discovering gram-matical constructions and drawing reliable comparisons remains correspondingly limited. And the few Etruscan loan-words found in Latin do not help us much further.

The Problem of Classification

This scanty source material has been subjected to such persevering and meticulous study that, in spite of countless disappointments and failures, enough understanding of the few more extensive pieces of written evidence has been gained for them to have become intelligible. Nevertheless even the celebrated mummy wrappings bearing an Etruscan text found in Egypt and now in the Zagreb Museum, the clay tile with writing on it found in Capua and now in the Berlin Museum collections, and the *stele* in Perugia do not, with their ritual directions and calendar formulae, really go farther than the rather circumscribed aspect of life revealed by dedications and inscriptions in tombs. It is in fact doubtful whether the Etruscans produced any kind of secular literature at all. It is true that we hear of a Tuscan historical work—the

Tuscae historiae—but this is obviously a later enterprise for which we have to thank Greek or Roman influence, just as the text-books to whose existence Latin writers bear witness seem to have been collected and systematically collated only in the Hellenistic period.

A variety of deductions and theories of origin have been advanced but to date no one has been able to identify Etruscan with any language spoken elsewhere or even, without doing it violence, to derive it from any other language. It seems to contain both Indo-Germanic and non- or pre-Indo-Germanic elements. Then again there are traces of certain peculiarities of ancient Mediterranean tongues, which appear also in the Lydian and Phrygian languages and of which evidence is found in inscriptions in the Aegean area, in particular on the island of Lemnos— and these tempt us to attach more weight to the tale of the immigration of the Etruscans from Asia Minor than Herodotus himself assigned to it. Links were also probably formed with the early Stone Age cultures of the Danube area. From objects excavated in Central Italy we can read the story of events and movements which took place in prehistoric times, but they present a similarly tangled picture and give indications of links with various parts of the world. Surely this is no mere coincidence! It may well be that the separate elements which compose this language reached Tuscany at different periods (for from the Palaeolithic era onwards the most diverse migratory movements and influences affected Tuscany) and that they were there fused by a long and complicated process into the Etruscan language which in this precise form was not spoken elsewhere and which resembles none but itself. Above all it remains for the time being an open question where and how in detail it acquired its peculiar characteristics and why just this tongue and not the Umbrian or Faliscan asserted itself as a unifying force in Tuscany whose population comprised such a heterogeneous collection of peoples.

3. THE CONFEDERATION OF THE TWELVE AROUND THE SACRED GROVE

A Confederation of Autonomous Cities

In addition to the written language there is a further proof of Etruscan unity, which must not be overlooked, namely the Confederation of the Twelve Cities, also referred to as *populi* or peoples. To understand this Confederation properly, one must bear in mind what has already been said about the nature of the ritually laid-out Etruscan city. The decisive features were not size or economic importance, but a sanctified pre-eminence above the rest of the world as a manifestation of cosmic order. Like constellations round the Pole Star, these hallowed places grouped themselves around the grove of the god Voltumna, the site of which has not yet been located but which lay in the territory of Bolsena, called Volsinii by the Romans and Velzna by the Etruscans themselves. It lay in all probability on the cone-shaped mountain Monte Fiascone, which can be seen from afar, or on one of the hills clothed in *macchia*[1] surrounding the lake which often gleams like molten silver. The attested bisexuality of the god worshipped here tells us that the cult was a very ancient one.

We can no longer make out with certainty which were the cities which originally formed the Confederation, for there is no unequivocal list and no definite conclusions can be drawn from such external attributes as power and prosperity. It is possible that the membership was changed from time to time in the course of the centuries without the structure being transformed. For example we may assume that another city took the place of Veii when it was conquered and destroyed by the Romans as early as 396 B.C. It appears that towards the end of Etruria's independence the following twelve cities formed the Confederation: Arezzo, Cerveteri, Chiusi, Cortona, Perugia, Populonia, Rusellae, Tarquinii, Vetulonia, Volterra, Vulci and Volsinii. The status of Falerii, Fiesole, Salpinum (which perhaps survives in Orvieto) and of Pisa remains obscure.

Even when in the course of his administrative reforms the Emperor Augustus expanded the system to fifteen member-states, this did not alter the basic structure, for the three new units which then joined the Confederation turn out, when examined more closely, to be simply parts of old Confederacy city-states which had become independent. Arezzo appears as Arretini Veteres, Arretini Fidentiores, Arretini Julienses, Chiusi as Clusini Novi and Clusini Veteres. It is very doubtful whether any more than administrative significance can be attributed to this new order or whether it caused any modification in the composition of the religious body which represented the Confederation at the shrine of Voltumna.

[1]Scrub, undergrowth, small bushes (translator's note).

Underlying Religious Principles

Our detailed knowledge of the Confederation is indeed slight. It is noteworthy that it was not known by the name of Tyrrhenian or Tuscan, but is referred to in official inscriptions as the Union of the *Rásna* or *Rasenna*. Every year at the appointed time religious ceremonies took place in the sacred grove of Voltumna. These included the election of the sovereign head of the Confederation and the driving-in of the year-nail in the shrine of Nortia, as well as prize fights, and acrobatic and artistic performances. People streamed in from every corner of Etruria to take part. The annual fair which coincided with the festival attracted merchants and all sorts of itinerant traders, who then bore away to the neighbouring peoples beyond the borders reports of all that was discussed and resolved at this assembly. For we scarcely need the testimony of Roman writers to tell us that on such an occasion conferences were held about affairs of common interest, such as how Greek trade was gaining ground, or the threat to the freedom of individual Confederation members, particularly from the enormously powerful Rome with her tendency to expand, but also from the Gallic hordes crowding in from the north. However, this was obviously never at any time the real object of the Voltumna festival or indeed of the Union itself.

In origin and structure the Etruscan Confederation was a religious alliance, comparable in many respects to the Greek Amphictyonic Leagues (see below pp. 48 et seq.) formed around Delphi, Delos or Olympia, though not to political unions like the Peloponnesian or Attic-Delian Maritime Leagues. This indicates its antiquity or old-fashioned character, for it was, in Greek terms, pre-classical. It never aspired to impose political, economic or constitutional standardization on the member-states, which were, as regards population, in part very mixed; never minted its own currency; and only exceptionally and somewhat clumsily launched a joint military action (cf. pp. 159 et seq.) The individual cities were free to form unions among themselves, or to dissolve them, as they judged fit, without prejudice to their membership: the Confederation itself was not affected. In the beginning it was a union of the priest-kings of the cities, the twelve *Lucumones*, who chose the Confederation's head from among themselves, and even after the monarchy was abolished towards the end of the sixth century B.C.

the control of affairs remained in the hands of the priestly councils, which seem at the same time to have been vested with certain judicial functions, similar to those of the Roman praetors.

The fact that the number of the member-states was twelve and was maintained at this figure with great tenacity, proves that the Confederation owed its establishment to some deliberate joint decision with a conscious aim, and to definite ideas of organization, and that we are not dealing with something which was the result of more or less accidental evolutionary processes. On the other hand this same figure twelve was so widely used as a basis for organizations throughout the Mediterranean area and even beyond, and its numerical characteristic of being three times four makes it so suitable for definition and division of time and space, that we cannot rely on it to help us to solve the question of the origin and date of the beginning of the Etruscan Confederation.

4. THE 'DISCIPLINA ETRUSCA'

The one thing above all others which seemed to Etruria's Roman neighbours to be 'typically Etruscan' was the so-called *Disciplina Etrusca* which the men and women of the leading families in particular had made their own. It was, along with script, language and the sacred organization of the Confederation, a further important factor which united the Etruscans and at the same time distinguished them from their neighbours.

Ultimately it was in fact written down in books but, as already mentioned, this took place only at a relatively late date. In what survives of it to-day we can recognize influences from Greek philosophy and Chaldaean creeds—showing how close was the relationship between the ideas of the late Etruscans and the world of Hellenism. In the *Disciplina Etrusca* were comprised all the religious erudition of the Etruscans, ritual regulations for sacrificing, prayers and divining, and in particular also precise instructions for the burial of the dead and for ascertaining the will of the gods from the shapes of the livers of sacrificed animals, from flashes of lightning and from the flight of birds. Every aspect of life was regulated by the 'doctrine'. In it were set out expositions concerning the calendar system, conceptions of time, distribution of land and the procedure to be observed when founding cities and establishing shrines. Some of it is ascribed to utterances of a nymph Begoe or Vegoia. The true founder and author, however, was held to be Tages, son of a 'Genius' and grandson of Tinia, greatest of all the gods.

Tages, Originator of the 'Doctrine'

The story goes that Tages, ploughed out of the field as a grey-haired child, chanted the doctrine to the *Lucumones*, who hastened up at the cries of the terrified ploughman. The *Lucumones* recorded his words and bequeathed them to their descendants as a precious possession. The miraculous being sank back dead into the earth immediately after he had made his revelation.

This story, like the closely related Erichthonius legend of the Athenians, belongs to the widely distributed group of goblin legends and admits of no inferences as to the place of its origin. One important point, however, is the close link with Tarquinii. The peasant who released from the sod this earthly child begotten of a spirit was driving his plough in a Tarquinian field and, according to the fragmentary reports, was called Tarchon. In ancient times Tarchon was already regarded as the founder of the city named after him, then later outright as the founder of the Etruscan cities, in logical explanation of the importance of the *Disciplina* for the Confederation of the Twelve.

In the tombs of Tarquinii intaglios have been found which can be connected with the Tages myth. On these instead of the child soothsayer a human head is seen emerging from the soil surrounded by rustics and priests with writing tablets. Such a picture clearly points to the characteristically Etruscan conception of the power of the head to represent a person and makes use of a type of Greek image of Orphic origin. Rings with gems of this kind may well have been worn by the members of the Tarquinian order of sixty *haruspices* (though admittedly the existence of this order is attested only in a later era) under whose hands the Tagetic books perhaps received their canonical form in the third or second century B.C.

When we consider how deeply rooted the Tagetic doctrine thus was in Tarquinii, it seems strange that the main shrine of the Confederation was not likewise to be found there but in the territory of Volsinii. However, a glance at the map reveals the natural link between Tarchon's town on the coast and Lake Bolsena, which lies a mere day's journey of twenty-five miles inland, namely the River Marta, which has its source in the lake and joins the sea near Tarquinii. Both from writings and from objects found in excavations we have proof that the Etruscans regarded springs and lakes as holy and worshipped them. The Lake of Volsinii then was seen from Tarquinii as the great and mysterious basin from which sprang the river. Relics found in Capodimonte and Bisenzio speak of the existence of traffic in early times through the Marta valley between the lake area and the Tyrrhenian Sea shore.

5. TARCHUNOS, PAVA TARCHIES AND VELTUNE

A Mirror from Toscanella

By this same River Marta, about half-way between the lake and Tarquinii, lies the little town of Tuscania (Toscanella). It is celebrated for the numerous articles of Tarquinian style found in the tomb-chambers and sarcophagi in its environs and for the two marvellous early Romanesque churches outside its gates, San Pietro high on the hill of the citadel and Santa Maria down in the valley at its feet, jealously concealed, as it were, from it by the Campanile, which broadly shields its rich façade. In the nineties of last century a bronze mirror[1] was found here, which, with its engraved picture decorating the back and the inscriptions carved round its edge, offers proof of the close relations already suspected between the city of Tarchon and the sacred grove on the lakeside (Fig. 8). Like the Athrpa mirror it affords us one of the relatively rare representations of the rich mythology of the Etruscans. It is possible that some mural in the ante-room of a temple or in a covered passage served as a model for the drawing which in its execution is a modest work.

A winged spirit like an Atlas bears on his raised arms the main picture which is drawn on the circular mirror back between two horizontal lines top and bottom. Above this the goddess of the dawn emerges, depicted as a woman's head adorned with a diadem, between the heads of her team of four horses. In the Etruscan mirror art of the third century B.C. these are conventional elements, but something special here is the group of five persons, standing closely pressed against one another, which occupies two-thirds of the lower part of the area of the mirror right up to the sharply upward curving serrated rim.

[1]In the *Museo Archeologico*, Florence. Inv. No. 77–759.

Fig. 8. The Tarchon Mirror from Tuscania (Toscanella), third century B.C., diameter 4⅞ in.

Scrutiny of the Liver

A beardless young man, bent slightly forward from the waist, is examining a sacrificed liver. He holds it on the hollow of his left hand in such a way that the large lobes hang down like pouches. The details of its shape which are important for foretelling the future are distinct. The fingers of the right hand are touching the surface. The back of the wrist of the holding hand lies on the bent knee of the left leg, which rests on a boulder, while the right foot stands at right-angles to the left, the sole flat on the ground. This is obviously the ritual stance for examining livers for we find it also on the famous Vulcenti mirror of the Vatican where the winged seer Calchas is represented contemplating a sacrificial liver.[1] (See frontispiece.)

His dress also marks the young man out as a liver scrutinizer or *haruspex*. He wears a short-sleeved undergarment closed at the neck, which is equivalent to the Roman *tunica*, and over it, on shoulder and back, a pleated cloak which reaches to a little below the knee and is held together over the breast by a large curved *fibula*.[2] The feet are uncovered. On his curly head he wears the characteristic headdress of these priests—a hat which rises to a high narrow conical top and, as we know from other illustrations, was held fast by bands knotted under the chin. Behind the youth's head the rising sun whose rays appear above an outline of mountain peaks points to the time as early morning, while the seedling tree sprouting out of the earth between three hemispherical stones and the boulder under the youth's foot indicate that this religious ceremony was taking place in the open air.

Above the young *haruspex* is written '*pavatarchies*'. This can be conveniently divided into *pava-tarchies*, which, in its second half, resembles Tarchet, the Etruscan form of Tages, though it is not indeed possible in the present state of research to say that we can arrive at any certainty on this point. If this picture was really intended to portray the founder of the Tagetic doctrine, then it must be based on a form of the legend which has not been found in any literary work, in which Tages was imagined not as a goblin-like earthly child, but as a youthful teacher. Despite the difficulty of adhering to this interpretation, the picture as a whole does seem to make it possible, especially as we find one of the other personages present designated in the inscription as Tarchunos, Tarchon. According to another interpretation of this scene, it does not represent the legendary instruction of the ploughman Tarchon in the new doctrine, but the liver scrutiny performed on the occasion of the founding of Tarquinii in the presence of the town's hero and of powerful spirits and divinities.

The central figure of the group is the youth with the liver. The

---

[1] Approx. 460 B.C. *Museo Gregoriano*, Rome. Inv. No. 1807. Length 7½ in. diam. 6 in.

[2] Clasp or dress-pin (translator's note).

manner in which he is displaced to the right out of the central axis of the area occupied by the picture, and the three heads at the left are balanced at the right by two heads flanking the sun's disc, together with the calculated rhythm in the disposition of the figures, all indicate the artistic quality of the model from which this mirror engraving was drawn—which may well have been somewhat more generously spaced out. It is intriguing to trace the various possible relationships between the figures.

Tarquinii and the Grove of Voltumna

Balancing the bearded man with the spear who is represented in a hero's nudity at the outside right, is the youth at the outside left, also clad in no more than a cloak slung back from his shoulders down his back. Beside him stands a bearded man in *haruspex* dress, corresponding to whom is the youthful *'pavatarchies'* beside the spear-bearer at the right. The five who are at the same time also six, can be grouped in three different ways. The youth and a woman frame the older *haruspex*, both standing slightly to his rear. On the other side the young liver scrutinizer and the bearded spear-bearer stand before and are amalgamated with the sun's radiant orb. Finally in the centre behind both *haruspices* appears the head of the female figure which, if one counts only the number of persons, forms the centre of the group. The eyes of all are concentrated on the complicated play of the fingers on the liver.

The bearded *haruspex* leaning on his staff is, according to the inscription, Tarchunos, Tarchon. He wears his quaint priest's hat slung round his neck and has his feet set in the same right-angled posture as his younger officiating or teaching colleague. The other three figures watching no less spellbound the liver scrutiny are probably *genii* and gods. The woman's name is, alas, a mystery, for the long undivided inscription above her is only partially decipherable. The name of Rathlth, given to the Apollonic youth with the olive branch, is otherwise unknown. But the powerfully built man with the spear at the right is Veltune, Vertumnus-Voltumna, the tutelary god of the Confederation of the Twelve and lord of the sacred grove in which each year the solidarity of the Etruscans was demonstrated in their own eyes as well as to the surrounding world.

Whoever may be the young *haruspex* designated 'Pava-Tarchies' or whatever the significance to be attributed to the liver scrutiny which he

Fig. 9. Back of a bronze mirror, the so-called Dorow Mirror, fourth century B.C.

is performing under the eyes of such exalted beings who are so attentive to his actions, the juxtaposition of the founder of Tarquinii with the god of all the *Rásna* on this Etruscan mirror from Tuscania confirms at least for the third century B.C. the close and fundamental relationship of the two and supplements what we know from written sources about the prime importance in Etruscan life of the Tagetic doctrine which had its birthplace in Tarquinii.

6. ALLIANCES IN ARCHAIC HELLAS

Amphictyonic Leagues

Every time we come across anything which could be called 'pan-Etruscan' we find it is without exception something to do with religion or worship. This fact struck the Romans and Greeks too, though they themselves were accustomed to attach great importance to religion which indeed imbued both their festivals and their daily life. Because the Latin word *Tusci* had a similar sound to the Greek word θύειν, 'to sacrifice', it was the practice to refer to the Etruscans quite simply as 'the bringers of sacrifices'. As late as the third century of our era the zealot Arnobius could describe Etruria as 'the originator and mother of all superstitions' because of her devotion to mysterious doctrines and cults. In a frequently quoted passage Livy said of the Etruscans that they were more inclined than other peoples towards religiosity and distinguished themselves by their art of giving to holiness a form in their rites.

It is probably in no small measure due to the peculiar social organization of the Etruscans that we have difficulty in understanding properly the spirit of Etruscan civilization and its mysterious and special position in the ancient world of which it was nevertheless a completely integrated part and to which it was so indebted. For the Etruscans were not in any way a homogeneous race, nor were they a people united by common ties of ancestry and language, or a nation, and they were not even primarily an economic union or defensive alliance, but a religious confederation, whose members were city-states of the western part of Central Italy, in many cases extremely diverse in origin and composition, each capable of creating its own history and working out its own development. Such a type of co-existence and relationship is not easy to imagine to-day and even the ancients found it more and more difficult to understand as they grew further away from their archaic roots. For the Etruscan Confederation of the Twelve survived into historic times as one of those obviously archaic creations which were throughout the ancient world so full of vitality in the eighth and seventh centuries B.C. but of which but a pale outline remains visible to us in the Amphictyonic Leagues constructed around the great shrines of ancient Greece.

The closest comparison available is the Ionian Confederacy of twelve cities, grouped round the worship of Poseidon Heliconius in the Mycalean mountains, in which, Herodotus tells us, four different languages were spoken and Greek and non-Greek elements were amalgamated. It is no more possible to determine why certain dialects in particular asserted themselves and why precisely the name Ionian persisted for the members of this league, than it is to answer the same questions about Etruria.

If ever the site of the grove of Voltumna is discovered it will perhaps be possible to give a definite date from which this shrine, which at first had only local significance, received its central status. When we consider the unifying trends which began to emerge with the so-called Villanova culture in the Early Iron Age, throughout central Italy, it is permissible to believe that the eighth and seventh centuries B.C. were the period of evolution which gave birth to the spirit of the people of the Tuscan cities and to many other expressions of vital and novel ideas in the cultural field.

Yet, though we may believe we see a sort of Amphictyonic League dedicated to the native god Veltha-Veltune-Voltumna in the region of Lake Bolsena, having its beginning perhaps back in the Villanova period, there was at least one respect in which the confederation of the *Rasenna* was sharply distinguished from the Amphictyonic Leagues of the Hellenic type. For, in contrast to the latter, the Confederation's members were not only bound by their creed to meet in the sacred grove at regular intervals but, far more than that, they were all devout disciples of a religious doctrine which governed every aspect of their life and all their conceptions of existence, and which was attributed entirely to one miraculous founder.

Orphists and Pythagoreans

Since spiritual occurrences and movements do not normally appear as isolated and rootless phenomena, it is reasonable to look around for something comparable in the environment of the Etruscans—to which Greece belongs increasingly from the eighth century B.C. onwards. The most obvious comparison is that with Orphism and the brotherhood of the Pythagoreans.

It can hardly be regarded as mere coincidence that we can identify elements in the Etruscans' conceptions of the Beyond which can be connected with the teachings of the legendary founder of the Orphic life partnerships. The links with the sodalities established by Pythagoras in the second half of the sixth century B.C. seem even more important. Members of the aristocratic ruling classes of Crotona and of other Sicilian and southern Italian cities joined these confraternities and submitted themselves in the conduct of their private lives and in their social and political aspirations to rules which the Master derived from his philosophical teachings and which he established with them. He himself became a mythical figure under the very eyes, as it were, of the historians.

Admittedly it may be a case of confusion between Crotona in southern Italy and Cortona in Etruria when Pythagoras is occasionally described by the ancients as '*lucumo*', priest-king, Etruscan style, or as Tyrrhenian. But the fact that it was possible to form such theories and hold them does indicate that real or imaginary links and similarities between the creations of Pythagoras and those of the Etruscan world of life and imagination were observed. Plutarch quotes the statement of a certain Lucius, otherwise unknown to us, whom he speaks of as a Tuscan, who is alleged to have declared that his fellow-countrymen still paid heed to secret signs given by Pythagoras to his disciples, e.g. the disorder in which the bedclothes were thrown on rising from one's couch. Ancient writers give some other indications that there were a few individual Pythagoreans in Etruria. King Numa, Romulus's legendary successor, who was, judging by his prowess as an organizer and formulator of methods of worship and of religious customs, a typical Etruscan, was reputed to be a pupil of the Greek sage, according to one of the most widely disseminated traditions. A late legend even related that Pythagoras was a brother of Tyrrhenus.

Since its rediscovery the splendid vaulted chamber on the slope of the city hill of Cortona has been designated the Tanella of Pythagoras and under this honourable name it has attracted countless visitors, but this is the result of compressing all the ancient observations, indications and misunderstandings into a kind of symbol. It is certain that Pythagoras was not buried in Cortona, much less in this vaulted structure of the fourth or third century B.C. Nor has this anything to do with the question we are here discussing, i.e. whether the Tagetic doctrine stands in a relationship of dependency to that of Orpheus or Pythagoras. The source-material available is far from being sufficient for any such conclusion to be drawn or even for any such suppositions to be formed. Nevertheless, it becomes easier to understand the peculiarities of Etruscanism if we can relate them to similar phenomena in other Mediterranean countries.

CHAPTER III

Links with the rest of the Ancient World

I. CONNEXIONS WITH THE COUNTRIES OF CENTRAL EUROPE AND THE DANUBE

Before the Era of the Cities

Etruria had been inhabited for tens of thousands of years before the people we know, and the ancients knew, as the Etruscans began about the eighth century B.C. to evolve their own distinctive civilization. The relics displayed in the prehistorical museum in Perugia range from the Palaeolithic age down to historical times. An eventful and frequently confused tale lies concealed behind them. Yet, though it may be true that Italic prehistory has not yet yielded up more than its first secrets, there is one thing which we do already know and that is how simple life was until the Iron Age, in the region between Florence and Rome, between the Tyrrhenian coast and the central Apennines, indeed everywhere in Italy.

There were no pyramids or towering temples here, and in this countryside there are no ruins of palaces or royal citadels, such as the Minoan and Mycenaean cultures bequeathed to Crete and Greece. Nor do we find in Tuscany any traces of a monumental architecture such as are to be found in Sardinia's still unexplained '*nuraghe*' or in Malta's huge rock temples. There was as yet no writing and an art which was either purely decorative or religiously symbolic was incapable of taking as its objective a portrait of man.

Nor had the time yet come when cities were to be established as the permanent dwelling-places of largish social groups stratified in classes. There is no place where one layer of residences is found above another as in Troy and indeed in the '*tels*'[1] throughout the Near East. The few

[1]'Tel'=artificial mound or hillock usually covering ruins of a city (translator's note).

single settlements and village-type enclosures seem each to have been inhabited only for relatively short spells and there is still need for research into the extent and type of stabilization which existed during the different periods and stages of evolution.

All this must be appreciated before one can begin to realize what it meant to Etruria when she began in the eighth century B.C. to establish closer relations and lasting contacts with the civilizations of the eastern Mediterranean and the Near East, and in particular with Hellas. It is largely from these that the special characteristics and the achievements of the Etruscans sprang.

Isolated discoveries indicate that here and there in Italy and most strikingly on the offshore islands contact with the Aegean world occasionally took place earlier. However, even if we were to conclude from this that crews of ships and small groups of emigrants landed and perhaps actually settled and even partially preserved their own speech, the fact is that in general, and especially in Tuscany, they seem to have had no perceptible influence. Navigation obviously had no great significance for the Italic people and they apparently also felt no inclination themselves to undertake any migration. It would appear, judging by the remains discovered, that all their links were overland and with western and central Europe, and particularly with the area around the middle reaches of the Danube and with the northern part of the Balkan peninsula. Apparently too this circumscribed area was not subjected to any strong influences emanating from Italy, and clearly Italy itself for many long centuries did not exercise any special attraction on other countries. At every period in world history there have been parts of the world privileged above others, on which all peoples cast a covetous eye because they offer wealth or living conditions which happen to be appropriate to the times. For a moment of history human evolution progresses more swiftly there than in other areas where life flows more quietly and is placidly making its preparations for the future.

The Age of the Great Migration

The position changes as the second millennium B.C. draws to a close. The whole Mediterranean area and beyond seems possessed by restlessness. This period is known as the time of the Aegean or Great Migration. The Empire of the Pharaohs on the Nile is attacked by the 'Maritime Nations' as they are called collectively in the Egyptian inscriptions: the people 'coming from the countries of the sea'. 'They laid their hands on the countries to the edge of the earth, their hearts were full of confidence: "our plans are successful".' The empire of the Hittites disintegrates. The fortresses of the Achaeans in Hellas crash in ruins and Troy falls victim to destruction a second time. Tribal and racial groups intermingle, then divide again, then join up anew with others. Now at last it begins to be clear what exactly is covered by the name of Illyria, a name which crops up in Greece and Italy and is also connected with the so called Lausitz civilization of the Late Bronze Age in Central Europe. It would seem as though the widest dispersion of all was attained with the Philistines in Palestine.

We have only partial knowledge of what is happening at the same time in the Far East. Mongolian shepherds from the Steppes, the warlike Chou people, overrun China and lay the foundation of a new chapter in Chinese history. From the regions beyond the Caspian Sea the Thracian Cimmerii groups come pressing into the Danube lands, into Asia Minor and into the Balkans.

An era of terrific turmoil now dawned among the nations. Worldwide movements led to encounters between races and civilizations which had evolved more or less in isolation. Conceptions of life, religious experiences and forms, inventions, techniques and arts were adopted, adapted and rejected. We do not know the precise reasons for this universal unrest. Deterioration in climatic conditions, which we know probably took place about 800 B.C. in the Alps and which seems to have forced certain settlements in that area to be given up, is not sufficient explanation. Everywhere the large and densely occupied cemeteries speak of sharply increasing populations.

One fruitful consequence of the encounter and cross-fertilization of ancient Danubian, Aryan-Indo-Germanic and Asiatic elements was the creation in the middle reaches of the Danube of a cultural centre which radiated a powerful influence in the direction of the Lausitz and towards Greece and Italy.

Bronze rings and belt buckles, decorative bridles and all kinds of jingling harness gear prove how important the horse was to these tribes. It is the horse-drawn chariot of war which carries the warrior quickly over great distances to the enemy. Riding, an art hitherto unknown in Europe, becomes popular, and creates a lively feeling of space, which had previously not been experienced in this way. The transition from

Plate VII.   Bronze bust from Vulci

(British Museum)

Plate VIII.   A hut-urn from Vetulonia

(By permission of the Archaeological Museum, Florence)

burial of corpses to cremation and urn-burial tells of a changed attitude to life and death, of hopes of resurrection and transsubstantiation, and a heightened belief in a strong individual life of the soul. Shamanistic ideas and practices, peculiar to the primitive Eastern peoples of the Steppes, seem to have an influence (cf. pp. 58 et seq.). A wealth of invention comes to light in bronzes and vases; everywhere there are signs of a delight in storytelling and in technical experimentation, in refinement and diversification of working methods, in creative variation of ornaments and shapes, and everything points to increased vitality and intellectual activity.

In Italy they speak of this time, the end of the second and beginning of the first millennium B.C., as a 'period of original creations'. Buried in these words lies a second fact, important in our context, namely that

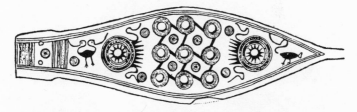

Fig. 10. Bronze belt from Populonia. Early Iron Age. 15¾ in. long

this cross-bred culture, charged with a multiplicity of strains and experiences, forced its way over the Eastern Alps as it did over the Adriatic, down into the Apennine peninsula. Here it released those violent stimuli and changes which were to find their outlet *inter alia* in the creation of the so-called Villanova culture.

2. THE VILLANOVA CULTURE

When articles all dating from the same time are found in excavations in any particular region and all resemble one another so strikingly that it is possible to conclude that there was some degree of homogeneity in living standards and conditions in that area, the prehistorians speak of a 'culture'. They usually give it the name of some place which has for some reason proved important to research workers but the fact that they choose this name does not necessarily mean that they have arrived at a decision about the origin, the type and the actual centres of this particular way of life. In every case research has to be undertaken to discover the extent to which language and tribal frontiers coincide with the limits of such cultures, and it is often difficult or even impossible to arrive at any decision on this point.

The Villanova culture gets its name from a suburb of Bologna, one

Fig. 11. Bronze helmet from Tarquinii. Early Iron Age. Height approx. 15⅜ in.

of the principal places in which its products have been discovered. The *Museo Civico* in Bologna possesses a collection of urns and furnishings so large that it would scarcely be possible to look at them all. The period the Villanova culture covers, from its beginnings in 1100 B.C. till the close of the eighth century B.C., corresponds roughly to that of the geometric style in Greece, which appears to have been nourished in part from similar sources. The area which it covers, however, extends far beyond Tuscany. It seems moreover that one of the most important centres if not actually the home of its rapidly advancing evolution lay not in the northern Apennines but in the southern Etruscan coastal belt, i.e. in the area of Tarquinii, Cerveteri, Veii, the very district which in the following era could be described as the heart of Etruria. As for its style, it seems to have a close relationship with the so-called Hallstatt culture of the Eastern Alps.

The simple, approximately knee-high funerary urns of the Villanova period make a fascinating impression. They are shaped as double-cones and the degree of their squatness or their slenderness is determined by their date in the period of development. The yellowish brown to deep black unpolished gleaming clay is porous and darkened by the smoke of the potter's kiln. Heavy and moist from the water they have absorbed, lumps of clay shaped by men's hands, these thick-walled vessels emerge from the earth. A single strong horizontal handle grows out of the wall of the vessel at the broadest point of its body, giving the product a peculiar vitality, rendered all the more striking by this asymmetry. The stresses of construction are emphasized by simple geometric patterns and signs, groups of triangles and rectangles, large squares filled with meander[1]-type broken crosses, punched circlets, dots and rings. These have all been stamped in or incised before the firing, and the white lime paste with which the deep grooves were frequently filled gives a sort of solemn festiveness to the whole. The shallow saucer with a single handle which lies over the opening like a cap set on askew completes the impression of primitive power.

These urns were buried in great fields, close to one another, but each set upright in its individual shaft sunk in the earth. It is unusual to find two one above the other.

The gifts laid beside the dead are in every case modest, as was life itself in Italy at that time. A scraper knife, trapezoid or half-moon-shaped according to the date, a couple of articles of clothing, and perhaps the metal clasp of a belt, a necklace or a decorative pin, a distaff, a horse's bit, a sword and a lance-head, a little jug and a drinking cup—for centuries there was scarcely anything more. But those who performed the funeral rites clearly attached great importance to having the skeleton complete, for when the bones were gathered up from the

[1]Meander=ornamental pattern of lines winding in and out or crossing rectangularly (translator's note).

funeral pyre as it ceased to glow, the remains of the ashes were all put into the cavity with the urn, to ensure that even the smallest piece of bone should be included. A stone or a pillar might be erected like a menhir[1] above the grave as a monument in a form which would assure continuity of life to the dead man.

Care for the Dead

Underlying all this is a belief that the dead will be transformed in the grave into beings of new and enhanced power, the idea that they are for the time being helpless as newborn babes, and must therefore in this interim period depend on the care of the survivors, while they are, as it were, germinating in the womb of the earth in order to sprout into a new life. On the manner in which one assists and treats the deceased depends the eventual outcome—whether one gains in them powerful tutelary divinities or conjures up dangerous evil spirits.

Conceptions of this kind swept in waves over Europe at this time, and were also influential in Asia. Possibly their birthplace was the Caucasus or Persia. The incidence of urnfield cultures, as they are called from their burial methods, indicates their path and the areas over which they were disseminated. Apparently the men of the Early Iron Age were stirred by deeply moving experiences which inspired them with a new understanding of death and the soul. One notable special feature in all this is the belief in the purifying and transfiguring power of fire. Such conceptions have found expression in countless tales and legends of smiths, in the stories of the 'little man who was burned till he became young', the reviving cauldron boiling above the fire, the Medea-Pelias myth. On the other hand it is in the initiation rites of the shamans that we hear of a certain dream process whereby the novice is torn apart and cut to pieces by the spirit of one of his ancestors and his bones cleaned of all blood and flesh. Only his skeleton is preserved and is then clothed in new flesh and blood and thus transformed into a creature which is lord over time and space, although it has a body. The head of the future shaman, which was cut off before this operation and set down at the side, sees everything which is being done to the body and thus retains a memory of the former existence and preserves the identity of the old and the new man.

[1]Menhir=a tall stone, sometimes as much as 65 ft. high, set upon end as a monument, generally of religious significance, in the later Stone Age. (German editor's note.)

Fig. 12. Urn in human form, so-called *canopus*, from Castiglion del Lago, approx. 650 B.C.
Height 17½ in.

Knowledge and experience of practices of this kind gave rise to new forms of funeral rites and the Etruscans seized on them and evolved them further. They offer an explanation for the temple façades and porch-like structures at the front of tombstones of the Hellenistic era, such as we see in the rock-tomb cemeteries of Norchia, Castel d'Asso and Sovana, or in the tombs of the close of the sixth and fifth centuries

B.C. in Populonia and Vetulonia, shaped like little temples with terra-cotta roofs and ornamentation on the joists. Obviously the people of central Italy took these ideas to their hearts with unusual enthusiasm, thereby creating for themselves a distinguishing characteristic which endured for centuries.

Later, in years on which history throws more light, the Etruscans were to develop the very characteristics which the Villanova people now revealed, such as the intensity with which they sought symbols by which they might represent their beliefs and their concern with death. This led them to develop varying modes of expression in different places, which underwent adaptations and could at any moment be replaced by other forms invented locally or noted abroad. We are in fact able to trace the boundaries between the territories of the different cities by their funeral customs and their tomb-styles.

In the sphere of influence of these early iron cultures the urn is a sort of hermetic vessel, in which a mysterious process of transformation and creation takes place; the connexion with present-day cremation and cinerary containers is at most merely one of form. The funerary receptacle of the Villanova era had to be shielded in accordance with a ritual, on account of the processes taking place within it, just as the medieval alchemist shielded his retort. The grave was surrounded by a circle of upright white stones and the urn was made safe by a stone in the form of a shield or roof laid on top of it, or by a helmet made of sheet bronze or burned clay.

Helmet–Urns and Hut–Urns

However, the helmet-urn draws attention to the fact that the funerary receptacle is not only a transformation-vessel but also the permanent form of the being who has become formless. Thus the urns in Saturnia take on a human appearance from the large head-shaped lids; the hemispherical cap-helmet of a cinerary jar in Tarquinii acquires a face, and in Chiusi the masks[1] bound on to the front of the urns turn them into those strange *canopi* with enormous staring eyes and arms affixed to or laid on the squat belly. There they sit, enthroned on clay and bronze chairs,[2] adorned with golden earrings and originally, as we learn from a few isolated discoveries, dressed like dolls. Urns of about the same age found in north Germany also have faces and are

[1]See Fig. 14. [2]See Fig. 15.

further evidence that this sort of imagery was the logical elaboration of the display which was a basic part of funeral ceremonies.

This is also true of the hut-urns (see plate VIII) which have come to light in southern Etruria and Latium and in great numbers in Vetulonia. They too have parallels in north Germany. They are a realization of

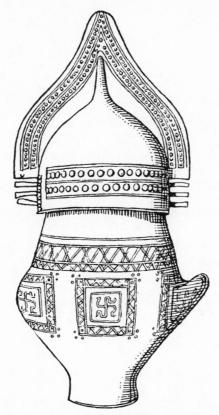

Fig. 13. Helmet-urn from Tarquinii. Early Iron Age. Height approx. 19¾ in.

the idea, so important in the evolution of Etruscan thought, that the house of the dead should be a copy of the deceased's dwelling; an idea which was most perfectly expressed in the tomb-chambers of Cerveteri and Tarquinii. This idea was not then new in the Mediterranean area or indeed in Europe, and was even older than cremation. Tiny utensils from tombs, to be seen in large quantity in the little local museum of Vetulonia, prove that the Etruscans, like other peoples, imagined the spirits of souls as dwarf-like and that they really regarded these little houses for ashes as the dwelling-places of the deceased.

Fig. 14. Bronze urn-mask from Chiusi, seventh century B.C. Height approx. 12⅝ in.

In these early creations, however, there is not only much variety but also much that seems contradictory. The Etruscans themselves seem to have retained as a basis of their views on life an awareness of the multiplicity of meanings which could be attached to signs and the possibility of *conjunctio oppositorum*—the conjunction of opposites. Tombstones preserved in great number from Cerveteri teach us that in this district the hut, the house, can be taken to stand for the mother's womb.[1] In that region they had the custom of setting in front of the mounds of the dead either little stone pillars as symbols of a man's procreative power, or little stone houses for the female sex, according to whether they were burying men or women. Women were even buried, in Cerveteri, on couches shaped like houses, while the bodies of men were laid on stone divans.

From time to time various different styles were fused, as in Veii where there are hut-urns out of the roofs of which rises a portrait head of the deceased, or in Vetulonia and Tarquinii, where the knob of the urn-helmet frequently takes the shape of a little hut-roof, or where the bowl-type lid is replaced by an out and out roof of clay in the style of the hut-urn roofs.

Burial of Corpses

In the Villanova culture we also find unburned corpses buried in trenches dug in the shape of coffins (so-called *fossa* burials) alongside cremation and urn-burial, but we cannot deduce from this a dualism of faith or even of origin. Attempts have been made to infer a contrast between 'cremating' and 'burying' Italic tribes, which might have immigrated at different times, or to attribute the differing funeral customs to Indo-Germanic or non-Indo-Germanic peoples, but the theories have all proved unsatisfactory and self-contradictory. The gifts found beside the dead have been too similar for it to be possible even to assume that the persons buried belonged to different social classes.

There was such a liberal multiplicity of forms and rites for cremation alone that it seems only reasonable to suppose that some special, more far-reaching formulae must have existed, which aimed at achieving the

---

[1] A *skyphos* of the second half of the fourth century B.C. painted with red figures, now in Boston (Inv. No. 973,72) shows a man and a woman saying farewell. Behind the man stands a bud-shaped *cippus* on a slender pillar; behind the woman a tombstone or altar in the shape of a house. Judging by the arrangement of the symbols the vessel may come from Cerveteri.

same object (i.e. the transformation and renewal of the dead) by other means, namely by prescribed sacrifices and procedures with the corpse itself. In fact, from the Villanova period right to the end of Etruscan history, cremation and burial persist side by side, each in turn being predominant at different times and places.

The Beginnings of Stabilization

There is probably no site in the country which was formerly Etruscan at which one cannot find the earthy, blackish-brown gleaming fragments of the former Villanova utensils. It is obvious that it was during the Villanova period that the inhabitants of Central Italy reached the degree of stabilization from which emerged the city life which then became a feature of the social organization and the colonization of Tuscany. True, there were smaller village-like settlements at an earlier date, but they all seem to have been relatively short-lived. Probably the method of soil utilization did not permit of lingering for generations in the same place. Cattle rearing may well have led to periodical migratory movements within limited areas: indeed reports show that as recently as last century herdsmen with pigs, sheep, cattle and goats still used to move, according to the season, between the Maremma and the mountainous country.

The early settlements of the Villanova people were also simple temporary villages of huts. Most of their dwellings, whose shape we know from the clay models in which they occasionally buried their dead, had a circular base and heavy roofs of straw or reeds, sloping steeply down. Anyone wandering through Italy to-day can encounter these here and there in remote spots, admittedly used only as huts in the fields or shelters for herds, or sheds for animals, but astonishingly similar in shape and construction. Rafters laid on top, and cross-beams set in a row one behind the other cross-wise over the roof-ridge, their ends carved as animal heads, give these structures of timber and mud a strange and to us somewhat sinister charm.

3. FIRST CONTACTS WITH GREECE

At the beginning of the eighth century B.C. these little settlements began to unite into townships, as did Rome, Vetulonia, Tarquinii and probably other places in Central Italy. Thus arose the type of architectural and social organization which in its Greek form we call '*polis*'

Fig. 15. *Canopus* enthroned on a chair, from Solaia, second half of the seventh century B.C. Height 29⅛ in.

based on autonomy in a limited area which could be easily surveyed and was bounded by natural contours. We have already spoken of the passion with which the Etruscans developed and preserved the sacred character of these communities.

It was just at this time that the earliest definitely known encounters with the Hellenes and their culture took place, as we learn from, among other things, the wealth of Greek utensils in the late geometric style discovered near Bisenzio on Lake Bolsena (cf. pp. 75 et seq.). This was the first important sign of the fruitful contact between the western part of Central Italy, and Hellas, which was just then opening up to the world. Etruria and Latium began to break the ties with central and south-eastern Europe which had prevailed till then and to become a part of what we now call the Ancient World.

For the moment, however, the connexions with the north-east, with the country round the middle reaches of the Danube and with the northern part of the Balkan peninsula were of decisive importance for the Villanova people. Despite diversity of detail, such a close resemblance can be seen among ornamental designs and shapes of objects dating from this period that it has been thought that travelling smiths must have been moving round the countryside, making helmets and shields, harness, pots and bowls in their own particular style. At all events it is impossible not to be aware that copper, and soon iron too, were being used and worked more and more. The ore fields of Tuscany were discovered and increasingly exploited. Although improved methods of soil utilization, developed in the far from exhausted fertile plains and hill lands of Etruria, were making possible a greater degree of stabilization, at the same time a second source of this new prosperity was certainly the abundance of ore and of timber with which to smelt it.

It was a convenient stroke of fate which contrived at the same period an extraordinary boom in Eastern Mediterranean navigation. Over-population, an urge to adventure and the struggle to expand their sources of raw material drove the peoples of the eastern Aegean into far distant lands which they had hitherto avoided, in order to secure from them, by force or by barter, grain and copper and iron in exchange for gleaming pottery, gorgeous metal utensils and gay textiles— all sorts of tempting wares. Greeks of mixed descent, Phoenicians and all sorts of people from the islands and coasts pushed forth into the unknown and hitherto timorously avoided west, towards the setting sun. They formed friendships and trade links, founded settlements or settled in existing communities as 'guest-settlers' and gazed with astonishment at the oddness of the foreigners. The 'Odyssey' is full of this kind of occurrence.

So long as in the main only overland routes were used, the ore from the mountains was, on account of its weight and unwieldiness, marketable only to a limited degree. It was navigation which finally facilitated exchanges on a larger scale and thereby created the connexion between East and West which was so important for the birth and evolution of Etruscan culture. We may well be reminded how Solomon's empire rose gloriously under similar conditions at the beginning of this same millennium. It took its place in the wider world because of the opening up of ore fields, increased sea traffic and more intensive cultivation, but its absorption into that world did not prevent it from developing an individual form of its own. Something similar seems to have happened in Tuscany and Latium towards the end of the Villanova period.

4. THE ORIENTALIZING PERIOD

Hellas in the Eighth and Seventh Centuries B.C.

Great changes were taking place in Hellas in this same eighth century B.C. It is variously spoken of as the age of Greek colonization, or of the poet Homer, or of the substitution of an aristocracy for monarchy or, if one is looking at the remains discovered, as the period of the Idaean or orientalizing style. In fact the bronze work and vase paintings, the designs of tools and vessels, the subjects of pictures are so very much determined by the encounter with oriental wares that it was only after decades of tedious analyses and meticulous comparisons that scientists learned to distinguish, beyond all doubt, foreign from native Greek articles. By these devious means they advanced to a new understanding of what was distinctively Hellenic.

We must not overlook the fact that no less an authority than Wilhelm Dörpfeld was still absolutely convinced that the new art-style and the new inspiration were the result of the encounter with the Phoenicians of Tyre and Sidon, which he believed thus laid the foundation of that evolution which finally reached its peak in the classic art of the Hellenes. However clearly the trained eye of the archaeologist may see the difference to-day, it is still in many instances very difficult for the layman without special help to distinguish the original works of the Greeks of those decades from wares and models imported from the Near East.

Etruria presents the same problem, but here the position is even less clear for there is a complete absence of written evidence such as the works of Homer and Hesiod and the statements of the historians and philosophers of the classic age provide for the similar period in Greece. And this was not the only thing which made a correct interpretation more difficult: every discovery which suggested even the slightest link with Asia Minor was immediately interpreted as a welcome piece of evidence to support the theory that the Etruscans originally came from Lydia or Phrygia.

Nevertheless, in the long view it was impossible, despite the admission of strong oriental influences, to doubt the independence and individuality of Etruscan culture. One of its main roots, the occidental, was acknowledged to lie in Hellenism and it was unthinkable to regard Hellenism as other than European. The discovery of ceramics and toreutics[1] in the orientalizing style or of daedalian plastics which make the non-expert think of Egyptian art, stimulated further investigation of the essential Greek.

There was no such enthusiasm for the study of the Etruscans, especially as their intellectual, political and military inferiority in relation to the Hellenes and Romans seemed to emerge plainly enough from later historical sources. Only a limited number of the necessary analyses of style and detailed research are therefore available. However, it is now possible to state in broad terms a fact which was valid for the Villanova period as far as the Early Iron Age civilizations of the Eastern Alps and middle reaches of the Danube are concerned: namely, that single objects and discoveries indicate an origin in this or that part of the Eastern Mediterranean region, Egypt, Phoenicia, Assyria, Cyprus and Greece. But so far, despite great efforts directed precisely towards this object, it has been impossible to find one large multiple complex, such as a closed cemetery or a settlement, which can be pointed to as a simple transference from another country and a continuation of a national way of life begun elsewhere.

[1]Toreutic art—production of objects of chased or embossed metal-work (German editor's note).

Why Greece adopted the world of oriental pictures and forms just at this moment of time, why the fabulous beasts of the East, sphinxes and griffins, lions, panthers and chimeras, now all at once began to encircle the sides of vessels, why coconut palms and lotus blossoms decorated bronze fittings, and why legends of gods and heroes became subjects for illustration, we do not know. Of course it may be said that the geometric style was exhausted and that some sort of explosion was needed if artistic life was not to sink into stagnation and to end in mannerism and demoralization. But what intellectual forces, what psychological turmoil caused this upheaval which seems to have affected every aspect of life?

We may ask the same in the case of Etruria. In an astounding intellectual and economic boom, the origin of which we can only partially determine or conjecture, a new feeling for life surged up in and was accepted by Etruria, demanding new means of expression. And the Etruscans found these means, as did the equally open-minded Hellenes, in what was offered by the contemporary Orient, and above all by those classic go-betweens of the Orient—the Phoenician traders.

Encounter with the Phoenicians

At the same time as the Greeks were beginning to expand along the shores of the Mediterranean, their so-called colonization period was also taking place: their struggle with the Phoenicians for factories, places to settle, bases for raw materials and export markets—if we may use such terms about conditions of those days. This caused Etruria to come rather within the sphere of influence of Hellas than directly in that of the East. Thus she absorbed the stimulating foreign products when already transformed by the Greeks.

The distinctive feature of the orientalizing period of the Etruscans seems to be the fact that various objects made by artists or craftsmen were imported direct from the Orient, at first in considerable quantities, and this can probably be attributed to the Phoenicians who came seeking iron and above all, copper. But this was quickly superseded by another wave of importation, this time from Greece, which at first sight seems very similar but on closer inspection proves to have been borne by different spiritual forces. These vessels, weapons, metal goods and furnishings were in their turn transformed to the Etruscan style of Central Italy. The Etruscans took them and adapted them, and in doing so achieved their own distinctive culture which the following centuries were to develop to perfection.

More original work from the Near East has come to light in the tombs of Tuscany and is displayed in the museum show-cases than would always appear from reading books on the Etruscans. Naturally for those whose aim is to comprehend essential Etruscanism, interest in foreign articles contained in tombs takes second place. At the same time the East itself, thanks to countless large-scale excavations undertaken in recent decades, offers such numerous and artistically such outstanding works of the most varied styles and periods that any objects found elsewhere and in foreign settings have generally acquired only complementary importance as works of art. Apart from the fact that they may be valuable on account of their beauty or curiosity, the value of single discoveries in comprehending Etruscan evolution lies chiefly in the fact that they can help us to fix dates, in so far as their relationship to the finds which accompany them can be established for certain. Admittedly this is rarely the case, particularly in the early excavations, and it is probable that even in recent times just as much information is continually being lost through secret excavations and black market trading.

It is usually relatively easy to determine the exact period to which an oriental work belongs, as written records and lists of kings begin at a very early date in the Near East and material for comparison is amply available. But the degree to which this may be of use to the Etruscologist depends entirely on the accuracy of the information available to him as to precisely which non-oriental objects he may, because of the circumstances of their discovery, definitely link with such a work.

Something similar can be said of the works of Hellenic metalworkers and potters in Etruria. In the museums and private collections of Europe and America stand thousands of Greek vases, detached from the surroundings of their origin, which were lifted from the cemeteries of Orvieto, Tarquinii and Vulci, and in the course of two centuries taken legally or illegally over the frontiers of Italy. When their value as products of Hellenic artistry is being assessed, the question of their origin, even where it is known, recedes into the background. Only a few people realize consciously that we owe to the Etruscans, the first 'Occidentals', the preservation of these works which they prized, acquired and laid in the tomb-chambers along with gold and bronze, as valuable gifts for their dead. No complete study of all these widely scattered objects has yet been undertaken from this point of view, and one could indeed not be made, since Etruscan research has been primarily concentrated on classical archaeology and on the difficult task of distinguishing the special achievements of the Etruscans from those of Greek and Eastern culture.

The Bocchoris Vase

One imported item which is particularly important in solving problems of dating in this period is the tall Egyptian balsam-jar of greenish faïence in the museum at Tarquinii which has inscribed on it the name of the Pharaoh Bokenranf.[1] Bocchoris, as the Greeks called him, reigned for only six years, from 734 to 728 B.C. and then, after several victories, fell in one of the battles he had to conduct against the Ethiopians. The king is depicted on the upper band of pictures in the company of the gods, while there are palm-trees, chained negroes and monkeys in the lower one. Similar observations elsewhere make it seem probable that this vessel, constructed while Bokenranf still lived, was put into the ground not very long after his death.

When the tomb in which the Bocchoris vase lay was opened in April 1895 its contents were found to be in disorder and in all probability incomplete. Grave robbers seem to have broken in in ancient times. At the date of the more recent opening up there were again alas! no scholars present so that it was not possible to record properly the precise positions in which the separate items found were actually lying. Later there arose differences of opinion even as to the contents themselves and the extent to which they could be regarded as complete or whether they had perhaps been supplemented by other finds. The scientific value of the discoveries is unfortunately diminished on this account.

In this particular grave lay many unequivocally native items, such as gold ornaments, *fibulae* in the shape of little horses on whose backs sit little monkeys, the fragments of a large spherical bronze amphora with impressive handles in the form of lotus blossoms, bowls of earthenware and strange jugs in bizarre shapes, and along with them some objects which are undoubtedly foreign. The ninety-one figurines of gods

[1]Or Bekenranef (translator's note).

made of Egyptian faïence seem to come from a neck ornament. A pair of whitish 'Bes'[1] figures, also of faïence, appear to have been mounted in sheet silver in Etruria itself and adapted for use as earrings. In other tombs of these times and even somewhat earlier date in Etruria, necklaces of Egyptian or Syrian origin, made of bright glass beads, and scarabs with hieroglyphs, have been found alongside such little figures. Side by side with items which were certainly imported from overseas are Etruscan imitations and adaptations.

New Wealth

How these treasures made their way from the land of the Nile to the Tyrrhenian coast remains in every instance an open question. In addition to Phoenician trade there is always the possibility of piracy. The wealth so suddenly manifested in a burial like this is in striking contrast to the former modest conditions. The woman buried in the Bocchoris tomb wore not only the precious objects already described but also a breast-plate of gold foil richly decorated in orientalizing style (see pp. 111 et seq.) as an ornament or perhaps as insignia of a priestess or a princess and her robe seems to have been sewn all over with little round and square gold sequins.

Inevitably at the sight of such royal garb and furnishings one thinks of the outstanding position which, according to inscriptions, illustrations and also late written sources, was occupied by women in the social organization of the Etruscans. Here in Tarquinii one's thoughts naturally turn particularly to the legendary Tanaquil, daughter of a *lucumo*, who procured the royal crown of Rome for her spouse Tarquinius Priscus and, after his assassination, for her son-in-law Servius Tullius.

The Bocchoris tomb is not however unique in its wealth. Gold and ivory gifts and bronze works of immeasurable artistic and intrinsic value have been found in other tombs of this period, and have indeed been the reason for their fame—for example in the *Tomba Regolini-Galassi* at Cerveteri, in the Barberini and Bernardini tombs at Palestrina, which are named after their discoverers, and in the magnificent stone-circle graves of Vetulonia and Marsigliana d'Albegna. Over and over again we find in the tombs examples of native arts and crafts

---

[1]Bes = Egyptian tutelary divinity, generally depicted as a dwarf (German editor's note).

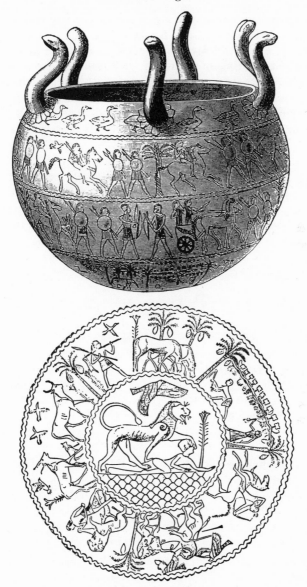

Fig. 16. Small gilded silver bowl from the Bernardini Tomb near Praeneste, first half of the seventh century B.C. Height almost 7½ in.

carrying on the Villanova traditions or imitating and exploiting foreign wares, and also objects imported from the East.

The Bernardini tomb lay in Latium, which, so far as we can determine, was at that time in no wise divided from southern Etruria. In this tomb was found a small hemispherical silver bowl,[1] on the bottom of which is a circular design, a drawing of a lion trampling on his human enemy while a Horus falcon hovers overhead. On the sides, surrounding this design, there are engraved one above the other four bands of pictures, delightfully alive:[2] the bottom band shows herdsmen leading their beasts, a peasant tending his vineyard, palms swaying, horses grazing. The middle bands are filled with scenes of hunting, animals fighting, and war, in a mountainous landscape, while at the top, in a long row, geese march in Indian file towards the right. Six snakes' heads, overlaid with fine gold leaf, rear up from the rim of the bowl: they are a later addition by some Etruscan master who thus adapted a Phoenician work to conform to Etruscan taste and perhaps to make it suitable for some specific purpose connected with worship.

The Pietra Zannoni

The so-called 'Zannoni stone' in Bologna[3] (Fig. 17) is a monument closely related to northern Syria in certain features; yet it is as a whole an individual creation, and despite certain clumsinesses impressive. It is the first of a long series of stone tomb *stelae* covering the period down to the fourth century B.C., decorated with reliefs depicting the dead driving or riding into the Beyond, which along with the Villanova remains comprise the principal treasure of the Bologna *Museo Civico*.

In the centre of the rectangular area of the picture, framed by a border grooved to resemble ropes, stands a stallion drawing a chariot towards the right. So big and powerful is the animal that the driver, who is by comparison small, makes an impression of insignificance as he sits under a sickle moon holding a long staff. Are we to attribute this to a craftsman's inability to realize proportions or is there in this a hint of the magic which surrounds the horse in the old rider cults of the East? Such a belief is known to have existed in the Villanova culture by the abundance of ornamental metal work on harness and bridles.

---

[1]See Fig. 16.
[2]Rome, *Museo Pigorini*. Height 5½ in., with snakes' heads 7¼ in., diam. 6 in.
[3]Bologna, *Museo Civico*; found in the Certosa. Height 24¼ in., width 36⅝ in.

How these ideas crept in from the same sources to influence Greece is shown by vases with illustrations of horses' heads and altogether the part played by the horse in Greece as a chthonian[1] animal in funeral ceremonies.

Unflinching, the gigantic man in the long-sleeved robe with biretta-type headdress grasps the reins of the prancing horse, in order to welcome or escort the guest approaching in the chariot. In later representations it is the demon of death who does this. Behind the horse stands a pillar crowned with wide-branching full-blown lotus blossoms,

Fig. 17. Tombstone from Bologna, the so-called *Pietra Zannoni* about 600 B.C. 36⅝ in. wide

and with a double-ringed *torus*,[2] perhaps a goal, perhaps a turning-column such as was used in chariot racing. The tall frieze of palm leaves and lotus flowers above the picture is of impressive force and can be directly related to oriental models.

5. EARLY GREEK EARTHENWARE AND POTTERS

Vases painted in the Greek geometric style found in the neighbour-hood of Bisenzio on Lake Bolsena (Fig. 18) belong to the very beginning of the seventh, indeed perhaps the end of the eighth century B.C.

[1]Chthonian = pertaining to the underworld (translator's note).
[2]Torus = moulding (translator's note).

They were obviously made right on the spot, but it has not been settled whether they were produced by the hands of a Hellenic potter or of an Etruscan who learned from models from the Greek islands.

Again and again this question has to be asked about individual works from that date onwards—not only in the field of ceramics. Related but later vessels have been taken from Tarquinian tombs. In the Bocchoris tomb too there lay Greek earthenware vessels and others influenced by Greek originals.

Fig. 18. Earthenware vessels with geometric paintings, from Bisenzio and Vulci, about 700 B.C. Height approx. 13¾ in. and 15 in.

Ceramics from Corinth

Beginning with the eighth century B.C. Etruria was increasingly flooded by utensils from Hellas. Countless numbers of proto-Corinthian and Corinthian oil phials and jugs were laid out beside the dead. Many of these, but not all, came directly from Corinth, which was just then emerging as an important maritime power. Many also will have reached Tuscany *via* the new, flourishing colonial cities of the Greeks in Sicily and southern Italy (in particular from Cumae and its predecessor Pithecusae on Ischia), filled with wine and oil and spices and bartered for ore and grain. The famous Chigi jug in the *Villa Giulia* in Rome, one of the most perfect and interesting vases in the Corinthian style, was found in the same chamber-tomb which lies not far from Veii, on Monte Aguzzo above the little village of Formello, in which was also found one of the earliest Etruscan alphabets, written on another vessel, which is known from the place of its discovery as the Formello alphabet.[1]

It seems that this sort of utensil was, from the time it was first encountered, imitated in Etruria itself as it was in other Hellenic cities. The Etruscans eagerly adopted the range of Greek styles and the Hellenic painting techniques which were based on age-old traditions.

The Aristonothos Crater

A large earthenware mixing bowl, which, according to the inscription on it, came from the hand of the Greek potter Aristonothos (Fig. 19), and the origin of which is not yet known, is, for this very reason, a particularly useful example of this period for our purpose. It was found in Cerveteri and stands to-day with other early vessels from the same place in the Palace of the Conservators on the Capitol in Rome. A study undertaken in very recent times by competent authorities and based on a wealth of comparative material demonstrates how difficult it is to make even moderately reliable pronouncements on origin and connexions in a case like this, and how one must take account of the most complicated cross-influences.

According to this investigation Aristonothos was a Greek whose home was somewhere in the Aegean archipelago, probably on one of the Cyclades. Between 675 and 665 B.C. he studied with an Attic master in the Cerameicus quarter of Athens; then he emigrated to the West. For some time he worked in Sicily in a Syracusan atelier, which in its turn had roots traceable to the Argive tradition. Ultimately, like others of his compatriots, he found his way to Cerveteri, where he established his own pottery. Once again he was receptive to local stimuli and his long years of travelling round resulted in his producing a work like the Aristonothos crater, the sole surviving inheritance bequeathed by a gifted Hellenic artist, who personified the restlessness and the intellectual receptivity of his age, and whom fate drove off his course to Etruria.

Above a double row of large chessboard checks, which seems to

[1] In Rome, *Villa Giulia.*

have been a particularly popular design in Etruria in these early days, illustrations containing many figures occupy the space between the two horizontal handles. On one side is a naval battle (Fig. 20), a subject which was as we have seen very popular with Etruscans of this era, when the sea was expanding, with its traffic, its adventures and distances, with trade and piracy and the acquisition of hitherto unknown

Fig. 19. The Aristonothos *'crater'* or mixing bowl from Cerveteri, mid-seventh century B.C.

wealth. A longboat, manned by warriors and driven by oarsmen, is approaching like a ferociously glaring beast of prey a sailing ship whose crew are preparing to defend themselves. The men on the two ships are not distinguished from one another by their arms, only by the type of their vessel and the symbols on their shields. The attackers bear geometric signs such as are already familiar from Etruscan illustrations of shields, while the men on the sailing ship have more naturalistic emblems—the head of an ox, a constellation, a crab. The same crab is repeated beneath one of the handles of the vessel. Are the warriors Phoenicians, are they Greeks, or Etruscans? Until fresh aids to understanding are available, e.g. the key to the symbols on the shields, these questions must remain unanswered. Both types of ships occurred then in Tyrrhenian waters, both will have been used by the Etruscans, and here, in Hellas and indeed among all the nations who sailed the Mediterranean, piracy was one of the natural ways of earning a living, like harvesting the fruits of the field, like hunting and fishing.

Fig. 20. Section of the Aristonothos '*crater*' from Cerveteri, mid-seventh century B.C.

The illustration on the opposite side of the bowl (Fig. 19) looks like loosely woven ornamental lattice work. Ulysses and his four companions are thrusting the spear which they have heated in the fire into the eye of Polyphemus. The latter, raising himself with difficulty on his left arm strives to push the terrible weapon aside with his right hand. The cheese-drying oven with the milk pail hanging on it, which can be seen behind him, framed and emphasized in an impressive way by the potter's signature in the right-hand corner, establishes the place of the action as the cave where the giant kept his flocks. The manner in which the approaching men are stepping symmetrically and nimbly on their toes, and are cradling the long pole with outstretched arms at hip-level, is sinister and fatefully purposeful. Ulysses, the last man in the row, only distinguishable from the others by the style of his movement, naked like them but for the sword hung aslant from his shoulder, is leaning backwards and pushing himself with force away from the cave wall by means of his raised leg, keeping the target in view like his companions and guiding the spear.

Homer and with him the Greek epics are beginning to become influential on Etruscan soil. *Inter alia* there is the rich carving on a famous ivory box of the end of the seventh century B.C. in the museum in Florence which was found in the so-called Pania tomb near Chiusi. It illustrates the flight from the blinded giant's grotto under the bellies of the shaggy sheep. In the *Tomba del Duce*, one of the stone-circle tombs of this period in Vetulonia, the bones of the deceased, which had been carefully gathered up out of the ashes of the funeral pyre, were laid in a silver shrine of the house-type richly chased in orientalizing manner. This was then wrapped in yellowish linen soaked in balm and afterwards enclosed in a heavy stone container.[1] Compare this with the picture offered by Homer's famous description of Hector's funeral, which closes the twenty-fourth canto of the 'Iliad':

'Dawn came once more, lighting the East with rosy hands, and saw the people flock together at illustrious Hector's pyre. When all had arrived and the gathering was complete, they began by quenching the fire with sparkling wine in all parts of the pyre that the flames had reached. Then Hector's brothers and comrades-in-arms collected his white bones, lamenting as they worked, with many a big tear running down their cheeks. They took the bones, wrapped them in soft purple cloths and put them in a golden chest. This chest they quickly lowered into a hollow grave, which they covered with a layer of large stones closely set together. Then, hastily, they made the barrow. . . .'[2]

There is much to make us think that getting to know Homer was one of the most important experiences of the dawning Etruscan civilization and that it had a perceptible influence on the style of living of the class of nobles which was then being formed and most of all on conceptions of the great gods.

[1]Length 26¾ in., width 9⅞ in., height 16¼ in.
[2]Translation by E. V. Rieu.

CHAPTER IV

A Royal Tomb of Early Times

I. VAULTED STRUCTURES AND THE CULT OF THE DEAD

The So-Called False Vault

THERE is an obvious link between the design of the Aristonothos crater and another earthenware vessel, scarcely less often discussed, but more than five hundred years older, the vase known from the principal figure decorating it as 'the Warrior Vase of Mycenae'. How this style survived, how it was affected by native Sicilian influences in Greek peripheral and colonial territories, and in Syracuse ultimately acquired the form used and developed by Aristonothos is a story whose details we know only in part. But we meet the same problem when we consider how the Mycenaean corridor design and *tholos*[1] structures are related to the vaulted buildings which make their appearance in the orientalizing period in Etruria—and here it is even more difficult to solve, even though the connexion itself is undisputed.

In these and the following centuries all vaulted structures erected by the Etruscans were of the type known as 'false vaulting.' The principle of the keystone was not yet utilized. Areas too large to be covered simply by the stones available were roofed over by laying each course of stones in such a way on the walls that it projected inwards a little over the one below and so, by the same process which gave rise to the coffer ceiling as an architectural style, the walls gradually converged towards the top. Depending on whether the space being roofed lies between two straight parallel walls, or has a ground plan which is circular or square, the person entering it has the impression of standing under a pointed arched roof or a domed vault. Both types of ground-plan are known in monuments of Mycenaean architecture: indeed, according to studies of the Bronze Age buildings in Sardinia and the

[1] *Tholos*= round building (Greek) [German editor's note].

early temples on Malta, it appears that they were used at a very early date throughout the Mediterranean area, and certainly long before the birth of Etruscan civilization. In any case the actual process seems to be such a natural one that it may well have developed spontaneously in more than one country.

At that time and for long after, so far as we can see, the Etruscans used this vaulting technique particularly in constructing tombs. Later the Tuscan, like the Greek temple, built of wooden beams, did without arches altogether; and huts and houses were also built with gabled roofs. The remains of the city walls of Populonia, Vetulonia and Rusellae, consisting of huge stone blocks which have a 'Mycenaean' look, do not date further back than the end of the sixth century B.C.: their gateways may well have had arches rounded like the entrance doors to the *Grotta Campana*, on the outskirts of Veii, which dates from the second half of the seventh century B.C., and is one of the earliest painted chamber-tombs of Etruria. (See Fig. 35.) But the only other way in which this technique seems to have played a part at that period is in a few isolated shafts sunk for wells, which broaden out toward the bottom in the shape of a pear and which are mostly difficult to date.

Arch and vault thus emerge as practical aids to overcome the difficulties of roofing-over buildings of dressed stone. They were not visible from outside and did not appear in the landscape as architectural forms, but remained concealed under the rounded grass-grown earth caps of the mounds whose shape did not actually bear any relation to the structure below them. Nevertheless, in considering the construction of these interiors it is permissible to speak of 'architecture' in the literal sense. For in the Casal Marittima tomb, built of blocks and slabs in courses one on top of another, which is to be seen in the garden of the Archaeological Museum at Florence (plate X), the evenly projecting right-angled courses of stone as they converge steadily towards the top produce a marvellous circular play of light and shade;[1] then there are the rectangular houses of the dead below the rock of the city of Orvieto, where each of the courses of stone projecting inwards consists of a short vertical bevelled surface alternating regularly with a uniting longer one, thus creating a most unusual and odd impression of a pointed vault. Then again there are the early chambers of Tarquinii and Cerveteri, in

[1] Height 6 ft. 10½ in., diam. 10 ft. 9½ in.

Plate IX.

A Tumulus at Cerveteri

(Photo: Alinari)

Plate X. Vaulted sepulchral chamber, Casal Marittima. First half of the sixth century B.C.

(*By permission of the Archaeological Museum, Florence*)

which the earthy tuff has been smoothed off to form widely arching surfaces which make the whole appear like the inside of a ship's hull lying overturned.

Arches and Vaulting as Sacred Forms

Apparently from an early date, if not quite from the outset, the dome and the arch were regarded as sacred and significant shapes. At that time indeed, because of their outlook and religious beliefs, the Etruscans were capable of regarding inanimate objects in a typically primitive manner as emblems of things beyond this world, able to affect men's lives. On the later urn-reliefs of Volterra and Chiusi, a door in an arch, tapering towards its top, became quite naturally a symbol of the entrance to the underworld.

In the centre of the impressive domed chamber of the Pietrera near Vetulonia there stands a pillar, as also in the Casal Marittima tomb mentioned above (plate X). In both cases the pillar, rectangular at the base and tapering slightly towards the top, reaches up to close under the centre of the vaulting without actually functioning as a support, because, owing to the method of construction already described, this kind of dome in fact maintains itself without a keystone and the support of the centre stone which closes it from below has therefore little significance in holding the whole in position. Later writers declare that it is possible to perceive in underground vaulting of this kind a '*templum sub terris*', the '*mundus*', a symbol of the world vaulted over by the heavens; and that cistern-type installations such as those found in the Nortia shrine near Bolsena were supposed to be shafts uniting the world to the underworld. The covering stone slab, the '*lapis manalis*' or 'souls' stone' could, as already stated earlier (p. 24), be opened only at specified times and in accordance with special carefully observed ritual precautions. Indeed the apparently purposeless central pillar in the two cupola-tombs named above points emphatically to such customs and theories; it is an image and representation of the axis of the world, which, according to ample evidence, used to figure in the religious conceptions and myths of the early peoples of Eurasia.

A comparative study of the diverse tombstone designs used side by side and on top of one another in Etruscan cemeteries, and an analysis of certain peculiar features of the artistic creations of the Etruscans entitle us to make such statements. The fact that a given meaning is obviously applicable only to certain individual tomb structures is no argument against the truth of these contentions. In the description of the Villanova tombs it has already (p. 64) been pointed out how, in a collection of objects at first sight unconnected, a certain trend of fashion can be perceived in individual cases influencing and transforming the form of funerary vessels and determining whether a single-handled jug with a bowl-lid was chosen, an urn in the shape of a helmet or a hut, an ash-container with a mask fixed on to it, or one in the form of a man like the Chiusi *canopi*.

Fig. 21. Rock tomb façades at Castel d'Asso, third to first century B.C.

The Great 'Tumulus' Tombs

In the seventh century B.C. a new conception of the meaning of life gave birth to two definite tendencies which made vaulted structures and in general the design of tomb-chambers outstandingly important. Each of the burial-mounds, often huge and measuring sixty-five and more yards in diameter, the Camucia of Cortona and the Pietrera near Vetulonia, the two Doganaccia mounds near Tarquinii, the Monte Calvario of Castellina in Chianti with its design of four tombs pointing towards the four cardinal points of the heavens, the Cerveteri mounds of the dead,[1] visible far and wide over the countryside, tells in its own way of a high degree of self-awareness. Homer gave expression to this feeling about life when he portrayed his heroes: a feeling which makes each man measure

[1]See plate IX.

himself, as though reflected in the mirror of others—his friends and equals—and build up his own self-confidence and strength from the wondering admiration of the surrounding world.

Tombs increase in size to accommodate the abundance of valuable gifts. In place of the former shallow trenches for graves come the mighty earth knolls above stone pedestals which may sometimes be coloured and may be decorated with reliefs or have sculptures mounted on them; or the tombs are hollowed out of the steep tuff cliffs round the cities, and great cubes and cube-shaped façades are carved out of the stones and fixed on top of them to look like monuments from a distance, as was done in Bieda and San Giuliano and in general in the rock-tomb cemeteries of southern Etruria. The tumulus-tombs and monumental box-tombs in the Cerameicus at Athens, the princes' mounds around Sardis, capital of the Lydian kings, and the mounds of the Hallstatt civilization in the south German foothills of the Alps and in southern France are evidence that this manner of valuing life, aiming at honour and posthumous fame, was known far beyond Italy and Tuscany. In this respect the Etruscans are seen to be a completely integrated part of the whole general picture of complicated interrelations, which are only imperfectly and somewhat one-sidedly embraced by the expression 'orientalizing era'.

Family Graves

If certain features are common to several peoples it does seem to be a peculiarly Etruscan requirement that spouses should ultimately be buried in turn after their death in one common mausoleum. This meant that a grave had to remain accessible for later interments and had to be of such dimensions that it afforded space for several burials. No one has yet systematically examined different types of graves evolved by the Etruscans from a sociological point of view; but it is plain that the matrimonial union of man and woman was regarded as an exceptionally strong tie lasting into the grave, just as, according to later portrayals of the Beyond, the fact of couples being united to one another was part of the conception of a higher existence after death. At the same time the manner of the lying-in-state and the accompanying gifts confirm the reports which say that Etruscan women, in contrast to Greek women, played a full part in public life and were the object of great consideration far beyond the domestic field. Later inscriptions indicate that children could bear the name of their mother alongside their father's family name.

We can infer a close unity and a strictly hierarchic order within the families of the great when we see how several tomb-chambers are joined together and arranged within one single mound, the central chambers belonging to the head of the family and his wife, while the ante-rooms and adjacent chambers are designed for the burial of further couples. Similar conclusions can be drawn from the arrangement of the mounds in Cerveteri, which all belong to one period and where around each of the distinguished lofty and stately 'mounds of the dead' smaller, less imposing ones are grouped. In the late Volumnia tomb near Perugia (second half of the second century B.C.), the central chamber with a pictorial urn of the head of the family, flanked by solemn winged figures, and an oil lamp equipped with several wicks hanging in front of it, acquires the character of a chapel by contrast with the other chambers. We do not know what was the relationship to the family of those interred in an ordinary way in the two adjacent rooms right and left in front of the entrance leading to the grave-house proper with its several apartments.

Finally, in addition to the reasons afforded by new views of life, another, practical reason was beginning to encourage the Etruscans towards vaulted structures, namely the fact that the new custom of inhumation began to predominate over that of cremation in most of the cities of Etruria. If the dead were to be buried lying stretched out on a bier, then the individual chambers would have to be so spacious that they would need vaulting-over for roofing. Later, during the Hellenistic era, the Etruscans turned again just as definitely, though still never exclusively, to cremation. This vacillation strongly supports the supposition that changes in funeral customs caused little or no alteration in essential ideas about souls and the Beyond, at that time any more than in the Villanova period.

Development of Building Technique

So it was that spiritual and technical reasons and general trends, as well as peculiarly Etruscan conceptions, all combined to develop an intensive preoccupation with the construction of vaulted buildings and their potentialities, such as Hellas never knew in this or the immediately following era: the wonderful achievements of the Etruscans in this field emerged at this period and persisted for years to come.

The Villanova culture had made a beginning, admittedly of limited extent but still enough to prove that some knowledge of the principle existed. Since it is clear that the funerary urn itself seemed to the Villanovans to possess great importance for the further life of the deceased, they must have felt it was important to preserve the urn whole and undamaged and to bury it in such a way that it would not be crushed by the stones and earth masses heaped up over it. To achieve this, thought and trouble were not spared. The solution of the task was comparatively easy where the earth in which the burials were to take place consisted of tuff or hard clay. A deep narrow pit—a *pozzo* or *pozzetto* as the Italians say—was dug and it was covered with a flat stone slab. But where the soil was not homogeneous and appeared to be much too yielding, another method was adopted. The urn for the ashes was placed in a larger earthenware vessel or in a container carved out of nenfro[1] or of limestone with a lid, which in turn was sunk into a burial shaft of appropriate size, or was placed in a relatively high vault, tapering towards the top, which was constructed of stones picked up in the fields. Typical of this last solution, which is an example of the beginning of the Etruscan vaulted structure, is a hut-urn grave found in the neighbourhood of Velletri: incidentally it is not unique.

The tuff of southern Etruria inspired and facilitated other types of construction. This stone is formed of baked volcanic soil, which hardens when exposed to the influence of air and with its relatively dependable firmness offers ideal conditions for making grottoes, adits and shafts, to-day as then. In this stone it was possible to hollow out, from above or from the side, chambers which were so broad that they provided space to accommodate two dead persons lying down, with a passage down the middle to separate them. At first the ground plan was roughly horse-shoe shape, with a straight, vertical framework for the doorways. Later the design became rectangular; the roof had frequently the shape of a shallow, almost flat vault arched symmetrically and evenly. The rock-tomb cemeteries of Bieda contain many examples of this style. Where the terrain made it necessary to erect structures of stone blocks wholly or partially above the ground, these were built as though they were underground. From discoveries in the territory of Tarquinii and Cerveteri we can compose a fairly straightforward

[1]Nenfro—stone of coarse-grained, porous texture (translator's note).

picture of their evolution step by step, beginning with the early tomb-chambers cut entirely out of tuff for the burial of married couples, with roofs reaching low down practically to the shelves on which lay the deceased; and going on to the chambers whose lower part is still in the earth and which are roofed with the so-called ship's hull vaulting such as the *Tomba della Doganaccia* near Tarquinii, still splendid even though it has already begun to fall into ruins again since its reconstruction.

In searching for means of dealing with the problem all that was known about foreign solutions was naturally eagerly studied. It looks as though every suggestion was seized upon—whether it came with immigrants (from Hellas and the eastern Aegean or even from Crete) who had personal experience in building vaults, or from voyagers who brought back reports of what they had seen in foreign countries, or from pictures on vases or descriptions in epics. That is why the individual shapes are so diverse and why it is impossible to fit them all into one line of descent.

The Cupola-Tombs of Populonia

On the shores of the Bay of Populonia cupola-tombs of the seventh century B.C. have been discovered whose internal structure has its nearest parallel in the Early Iron Age burial grounds of Arcades and Cofina on Crete. The chamber walls start with a section rising perpendicularly from an almost square ground plan. By means of filling up with spandrels which broaden and deepen symmetrically upwards in the four corners, the space laid out in cube shape is transformed into a regular circle and the whole is finally vaulted over. The vertical walls are composed of oblong sandstone blocks cut with right-angled edges and corners put together without mortar, but for the vaulting only hard, coarsely dressed limestone slabs were used.

It is plain that, as in Crete, this construction is ultimately based on the Minoan-Mycenaean *tholos* structures of the second millennium B.C., of the type of the so-called Atreus tomb near Mycenae. But it is possible also that, just as the design of the Warrior Vase persisted down to the time of Aristonothos, so this method of building survived also outside of Crete in some peripheral or colonial territory which was less affected by the main development. In addition to similarities between the form of the ground plan, the vaulting technique and the short low entrance to these tomb-chambers and those observed in Arcades and Cofina, there is the noteworthy fact that in Crete as in Populonia cremation and burial were carried on simultaneously. Yet on the other hand there are also important differences between the two types of tombs.

For example the tomb-chambers of Populonia no longer have their bases in the earth, but are constructed independently on top of it. In place of the mound composed entirely of earth there is first a sort of stone pedestal, almost the height of a man, in the form of a circle of perpendicular walls and these walls are finished off with widely projecting drip slabs on top of which, like a rounded shield, lies a covering of earth which is only relatively slightly vaulted. The same brownish-yellow sandstone blocks are used for this 'drum' as for the perpendicular partitioning walls inside, while the drip slabs and the paving surrounding are both of limestone. Finally in the interior, and this again is very different from Arcades, there stand high stone chests whose sculptured corner posts indicate that they are copies of couches, on which the dead used to be laid in couples.

The difficulty of differentiating between indigenous developments and foreign importations is plain enough, especially as it is only in the case of Populonia that a few older finds provide positive links with Sardinia, the classical country of early *tholos* and vaulted structures. In Vetulonia, Populonia's southern neighbour, there is a burying place, the Pietrera, which was constructed in the manner of the cupola-tombs just described, but which was too large and collapsed very shortly after it was completed. Unsuitable building material had been used, not capable of supporting a great weight. It was rebuilt immediately after the catastrophe in the same style, but this time of firmer stone. It is perhaps permissible to conclude from this that the builders were foreigners who were not sufficiently familiar with the qualities of the local stone. But it is equally possible that they were Etruscan workmen who, without direct experience of their own, sought to build here a copy of a foreign, perhaps a Cretan model, according to measurements which, like the site, which is visible from a great distance, had been determined by the self-conceit of the princely owner of the property.

2. CARRIAGES AND THRONES

The 'Tomba Regolini-Galassi'

It is no easier to determine whether there is a direct or indirect connexion between the Mycenaean fortress corridors and the *Tomba*

Regolini-Galassi. This is a corridor-tomb near Cerveteri, over fifteen yards long, also built with the technique of the false vault but with a steeply gabled roof. To-day it lies like countless tomb-chambers of Etruria empty and seldom visited, occasionally used by the peasants

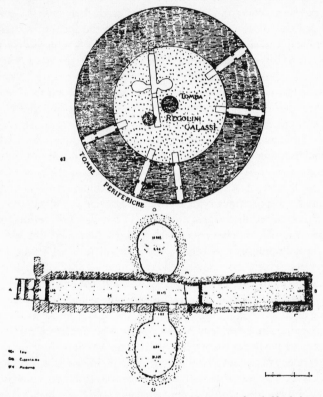

Fig. 22. Plan of the *Tomba Regolini-Galassi* near Çerveteri, first half of the seventh century B.C.

living nearby as a cool cellar for storing wine and fruits of the field (Fig. 23).

The Regolini-Galassi tomb was originally designed as a high and narrow chamber of the dead, nearly 24 ft. long and between 4 ft. 3 in. and 4 ft. 7 in. broad, partly cut like a trench out of the tuff where it stood and partly constructed of layers of huge tuff blocks. It was covered over by a not particularly large mound and entered through a straight open corridor over 31 ft. long. Within lay buried on a catafalque of stone a royal lady, surrounded by fabulously rich gifts, whose name, according to the inscriptions[1] on her silver utensils, was Larthia.

As in so many Etruscan tomb-chambers there were also two smaller burial spaces carved right and left out of the corridor wall immediately before the tomb-chamber. In this particular tomb these were a sort of rounded niches and a noble warrior was interred in the one situated on the right as you enter. In contrast to the princess he had been cremated and his remains placed in an earthenware urn. So we see corpse-inhumation and cremation side by side as a matter of course. It is a subject of controversy whether the warrior's tomb or that of Larthia was occupied first.

The third burial place is more recent than these two. It also contains extremely valuable gifts. For this the entrance formerly used was vaulted over in the usual manner and after the dead person had been brought in the mound was so extended and heightened that the entrance lay blocked and at some later date it was possible to construct another five separate chamber-tombs in the same burial mound. In the ante-chamber, as the corridor in its new form must be called, the corpse of a man whom many take to have been the son of Larthia, lay on a bier; she is thought to have occupied the royal throne of Cerveteri before her son.

In contrast to the right-hand side-niche with the warrior's urn the left-hand one seems not to have been used as a burial place but as an additional space allocated to the person buried in the ante-chamber. It is uncertain whether it was planned or laid out as part of the original design, whether it dates only from the remodelling of the whole or whether it was perhaps reconstructed at that time.

Anyone who wishes to gain an impression of the abundance and diversity of the gifts laid in the tombs of people buried with such expense in the orientalizing era, should visit the second gallery of the *Museo Gregoriano* in the Vatican Museums in Rome. There he will see the most important items from the Regolini-Galassi tomb and its immediate surroundings, found untouched when it was opened in 1836. They are clearly displayed and are made intelligible to the non-expert by explanatory notices.

[1]See Fig. 25.

Fig. 23. The Regolini-Galassi tomb near Cerveteri, first half of the seventh century B.C.

Carriages as Funerary Gifts

The centre of the festive gallery with its gaily-painted coffer ceiling and coloured frescoes is dominated by two high-wheeled chariots with bronze fittings. One of these is a four-wheeled vehicle without an axle, which, with its flat body, makes us think irresistibly of the later funeral carriages found in the Celtic tumulus tombs of the northern Alpine foothills. Its high narrow fellies are mounted with thick nail heads close to one another. A band of copper with palm leaf design which runs for half the length of the carriage vividly suggests the glittering splendour of such princely vehicles.

We may assume with some degree of certainty that the dead person was once brought on this same carriage to his resting-place beyond the southern border of the city, the more so as the deeply-worn carriage tracks in the tomb streets between the mounds of the Banditaccia are striking proof that this was the custom in Cerveteri. The bronze couch, slightly over 6 ft. long and slightly under 29 in. broad, just fits into the body of the carriage. It may well have stood on the flat-bottomed carriage during its journey 2,600 years ago as it does now in the museum. In the tomb itself the two stood separate from one another. Whereas the carriage was set up at the entrance against the wall to the left, the *clinia*[1] was found at the right, in the background, directly in front of the partition dividing the main chamber from the ante-room. A net-like lattice-work of bronze strips is stretched over the frame supported by six sturdy legs strengthened at their tops like pillars with capitals. Probably a thick mattress lay over this, similar to that over the catafalque of Larthia, the remains of which were found by the excavators. The deceased lay stretched out, his feet towards the exit, like the figures reclining solemnly on the covers of sarcophagi and urns of later date, when people were buried in stone and earthenware coffins and a permanent effigy of the perishable corpse was set on top.

The second carriage in the centre of the Regolini-Galassi gallery, whose long shaft, ending in a lion's head, points towards the entering visitor, is a so-called *biga*. This is not a hearse but a smart vehicle for everyday purposes, fit for the use of a distinguished man when he drove out over the country, to visit friends, to attend religious ceremonies or even to go to battle. It is a compact heavy chariot for one or two men, on powerful four-spoke wheels, intended to be drawn by two horses. This vehicle together with various weapons was given to the warrior interred in the right-hand chamber and it was partially burned, partly broken and taken to pieces to enable it to fit into the cramped niche. The rich metal mountings, ornamented with rows of palm leaves, remind us that according to ancient reports the triumphal chariot of the Roman generals, drawn by white horses, had its origin, like the custom of the 'triumph' itself and the rites associated therewith,

[1]Clinia= couch (translator's note).

in Etruscan forms of worship (cf. p. 127). Remains of carriages have been found in many tombs of this period in Tuscany, in Vetulonia, Populonia and Perugia. On Etruscan tombstones and urn-reliefs from Bologna and Volterra deceased persons, men or women, are portrayed travelling in a carriage into the Beyond.

On the wall above the two doors in the background of the Regolini-Galassi gallery in the museum there are two murals in bright yellow and green, which are taken from original drawings by Luigi Canina (1795–1856) who with exemplary speed gave publicity to the then newly opened tomb in his own richly illustrated book which was a pioneer work of Etruscan research just then beginning to stir in Europe. His descriptions of the ancient Caere and of the Regolini-Galassi excavations form a priceless source for the reconstruction of the discovery, even though the rather primitive methods of those days, and the desire of the excavators to get as quickly as possible to the treasures, prevented an adequately careful record being made of the conditions as they were found and therefore incidentally caused many inaccuracies, errors and misunderstandings in Canina's work. One of the murals depicts the complex of the mounds long since rendered unrecognizable by agricultural utilization of the land and as a result of archaeological investigations, the other shows this complex in the setting of a panorama of Cerveteri in the year 1836. Corresponding to these murals we find on the entrance wall, which the visitor notices only on looking back, reproductions of the cross-section and plan of the tomb, and beside it, particularly interesting and enlightening, the original arrangement of the relics sketched by Canina.

The Chair of State

In the first show-case at the right stands the mighty chair which in all probability came out of the main chamber, along with its box-shaped low footstool. Because the chair was almost completely clothed by sheet bronze which must formerly have glittered like gold but is now coated with a dark-green patina, its form has been preserved and it was possible to gain from the bronze remains an idea of the original shape and measurements and thus this very convincing reconstruction was possible.

Rich beaten work, prancing lions and stags and plants in the orientalizing style, decorate the top of the back rest and the box-shaped support of the seat. The two front legs curving slightly inwards

Plate XI.   A small cupola tomb at Populonia dating from the seventh century B.C.

(By courtesy of Kohlhammer Verlag, Stuttgart)

Plate XII.   The Tomb of Shields

(Reproduced by courtesy of Thames and Hudson from Pallottino: The Art of the Etruscans)

terminate in animal feet. Right and left horse *protomes*[1] spring from the front edge of the seat and the small arm-rests both end in bronze boxes each decorated with a sculptured poppy-head. The rectangular space between the boards which frame the back-rest would have been up-holstered with fabric or leather, as would the seat.

In Etruscan conceptions the throne played an important role as symbol of dignity and power. It is sufficient to point to the *sella curulis*, the ivory chair of honour of the Roman councillors, which in Rome itself was regarded as being inherited from the Tuscans. Among the exhibition pieces in Olympia there stood in olden days a throne which was alleged to be dedicated by an Etruscan king of whom we know nothing further than that his name was Arimnestus, and he was said by Pausanias to be the first non-Greek to bring a ceremonial gift to the Olympian Zeus. The Chiusi *canopi* were buried on chairs made expressly for them of bronze or burned clay. It is probable, moreover, that a special significance was attributed to the armchair in the religious ceremonies connected with the dead.

A clumsy dummy chair in the style of the Regolini-Galassi throne is carved out of the tuff immediately to the right of the entrance of the *Tomba Campana* situated on Monte Abetone near Cerveteri. It is part of the equipment of the front third of a spacious funeral hall which seems to have served as a sort of ceremonial ante-room. Similarly the rounded armchair of the Chiusi *canopi* appears in other early chamber-tombs of Cerveteri.[2]

To-day the best known and most impressive example is the *Tomba degli Scudi e delle Sedie*, the tomb of the shields and armchairs, which also belongs to the seventh century B.C. A broad hall lies in front of the three chambers of the dead ranged symmetrically side by side, each designed for a married couple. Around the walls of the hall six stone couches, of the type normally used to bury men, are evenly distributed. But left and right of the door leading to the centre chamber, opposite the entrance, stand two heavy round armchairs each with a foot-rest of tuff. Could it be that here in the ante-room the women were buried on thrones in contrast to the men and to the usual custom in the marriage chambers? What were the relationships of those buried here to the inmates of the chambers, and why are there only two chairs

[1]Protome = foremost or upper half, bust (translator's note).
[2]For illustration of a *canopus* see Fig. 15.

corresponding to six couches? Were funerals carried out here at all or did this hall-like ante-room, whose walls are decorated all round, even above the two thrones, with great circular shields carved out of the tuff, serve for specific ceremonies connected with the interment of the dead? We do not know, but the last suggestion is the most probable.

3. RELIGIOUS CEREMONIES AND OBSEQUIES

Masks of the Dead

There are three strange clay statuettes of ceremonially seated persons —one of a man in the Conservators' Palace in Rome and two of women in the British Museum, all dating from about 600 B.C.—which originate from Cerveteri. According to the rather inaccurate notes made at the time of their discovery they are alleged to have been sitting on little miniature armchairs like the five which can still be seen side by side in the *Tomba delle Cinque Sedie*, at the entrance to the Banditaccia. Perhaps in the *Tomba degli Scudi e delle Sedie* models of the dead, made of perishable material, sat on the life-size thrones and sculptured effigies of the dead lay on the benches around, as on later sarcophagi. On the other hand it is also possible that the deceased themselves were enthroned on these chairs during the funeral ceremonies. The little we have been able to establish about Etruscan ceremonies for the dead, handed down to us on monuments, is scarcely enough to give us a hint of what really happened. The manner in which the *canopi* were interred at Chiusi, and what we learn about a masque performed in Rome around the dead as they lay in state on biers in order to conjure up the ancestors, both have many characteristics of a magic puppet play.[1]

The Romans prepared life-like masks of their honoured dead, which they preserved in wooden shrines in a place of honour in their houses. About the middle of the second century B.C. the Greek historian Polybius reports in detail and with wonderment, how at public funeral ceremonies in the Forum these masks were put on to people 'who most resemble them in size and otherwise in outward appearance. These persons then put on the [appropriate] dress—the consul or praetor the purple-edged toga, the censor the purple one, the victor the gold-

[1]The famous 'Warrior of Capestrano' in the *Villa Giulia* in Rome represents a warrior prepared for funeral ceremonies: standing between two supporting pillars, with a mask, official robes and insignia of office, just as Polybius says was customary for Roman funeral ceremonies in the Forum.

embroidered one. Then they drive in their carriages; rods, axes and whatever else is fitting to the particular offices are carried before each of them according to the rank which each had attained in his lifetime. When they come to the Rostra they all sit down in a row on ivory chairs. . . .' The deceased himself, as Polybius has previously informed us, is personally set up here in his array, or is in rare cases reclining on a bier. 'Who would not be moved to see the likenesses of these men, so highly esteemed for their valour, all as though they were alive and breathing? Moreover the orator on whom it has devolved to speak of the person about to be buried—a son who is old enough to do so, or a near relative—now begins, when he has finished the funeral oration, to recount the works and deeds of all present, beginning with the most senior.'

Funeral Ceremonial

In recent times Hittite texts have been found, which, though they date from as far back as the fourteenth or thirteenth century B.C., sound as though they were explanations of many of the early conditions which have come to light in Cerveteri and elsewhere in Etruria. After his death a king or a queen is cremated and in the ceremonies described there are clearly influences which spring from an earlier date when cremation was still unknown. The principal feature is that the mighty dead person by means of a complicated process, 'becomes God', just as it is told of the Etruscans that they knew how to make the souls of their dead divine by means of the blood of specific animals. Accompanied by the lamentations of the great of the land the body of the departed is borne on a truck out to a place where a tent has been erected in which he lies in state, while food is set before him and sacrificial drinks brought. The details of the cremation remain unclear, but at sunrise the women come to the funeral pyre which has now burned low. They extinguish the last flames with ten jugs of beer, ten jugs of wine and ten jugs of 'walki'. They gather the bones with a silver spoon into a silver vessel of prescribed size which is filled with fine oil, then take the bones out again and lay them on linen and finely woven fabric. Then they place them on a throne if the deceased was a man, on a stool if a woman.

Around the site of the fire are laid twelve loaves of bread over which a fatty broth is then poured. A table is placed before the chair on which lie the bones of the deceased, and bread is broken. Specially appointed people lay out plates and all who took a part in the gathering of the bones then enjoy a funeral feast. Three times something to drink is given to them, and the same number of times to the soul of the dead person. Then comes a strange procedure which the condition of the extant text makes it difficult to understand. A sort of figure of a man is made of raisins and olives, with other fruits added as well as sheep's wool, and into this doll intoxicating drinks are poured and bread is stuffed. A dialogue between an old woman and her companion play a part, and a pair of scales, one of which is filled with jewels, the other with something not yet interpreted. Sheep and oxen are sacrificed to the sun, to the earth and to the soul of the deceased. Finally the bones, together with the chair on which they lie, are carried to 'their stone house' where they are then taken off the throne and laid out as though they were the unburned body, on a couch in front of which a lamp filled with fine oil is placed. Ceremonial sacrifices follow which last for days.

In view of our remoteness from the period we are examining and the absence of comparable details as well as the lack of corresponding accounts for Etruria, one is reluctant to draw any conclusions about the origin of the inhabitants of Cerveteri or of Chiusi from these reports. Yet it is important just to have some idea of the kind of customs we have to reckon with even though we can no longer be conclusive about them from the remains found. If ever it appeared probable that there really were links over and above these, then it would provide additional confirmation of the theory that Hittite ancestry can be traced among the Etruscans in this period of improved communications in the Mediterranean and of the orientalizing style in art with Egyptian, Phoenician and Assyrian elements and inspiration and so many of the very influences which had such a formative effect on the religion of Greece. Moreover, everything that can be deduced from the great variety of types of tombs and funeral rites in Etruria during the centuries of its independent history proves the Etruscans' readiness to experiment, because of the intense fascination which death and existence in the Beyond had for them—a characteristic scarcely found anywhere else. They were always on the look-out for effective means to assure to their dead some life and promotion in the Beyond so they adopted inspiration from every source; they elaborated ideas, amalgamated foreign elements with their own notions, then gave them up and repudiated them in order to seize on something new or resume some former practice.

In the Hittite ritual the deceased appears as host. Those who gathered up his remains from the funeral pyre hold a funeral feast in front of his bones raised up on to the throne, a feast in which he himself takes part and drinks intoxicating liquors. It is obvious that the Etruscans had similar ideas. It is appropriate to the enhanced existence of the dead man that he should eat and drink together with his wife and his friends in the circle of his forefathers, should listen to the musicians and take pleasure in the displays of jugglers and dancers and in the contests of athletes. This is what many of the murals in Tarquinii and Chiusi depict from the sixth century B.C. onwards.

Near Orvieto was found the *Tomba Golini*, a tomb-chamber of the end of the fourth century B.C. A mural painting from this tomb was brought to the Archaeological Museum in Florence. It depicts the preparation of such a banquet. Servants and wineservers are rushing busily around. On the ornate tables resting on long legs which end in animals' feet stand drinking bowls, mixing vessels and jugs of different sizes and shapes, a whole dinner service. Here at the kitchen-stove baking and cooking are going on, there someone is kneading dough in a big basin, and on one of the projections of a tree whose branches have been cut off hangs a whole ox cut open. Its bloody head, parted from the torso, is lying on the ground near by. Candles, fixed in high candelabra shaped like birds' heads, throw a festal light over the underground chamber. Eita, Lord of the Underworld, the host himself, wearing a wolfskin as a cap, ceremoniously enthroned with his spouse Persipnei, awaits the deceased, who approaches on a *biga* drawn by swift and fiery horses. He is being received by a winged female figure, a Lasa, who bears in her right hand a scroll inscribed with a record of his deeds. The dead members of his family, the family of the Velia, are already gathered for the feast. Over the door stands the watchman with a great curved trumpet.

4. BRONZE FURNISHINGS
Cauldrons and Bowls

Even in the orientalizing period all the furnishings necessary for such a feast were supplied to dead noblemen. So abundant was the equipment that the tomb-chambers could scarcely accommodate it all even after they became more spacious. The great quantity of crockery and cutlery of earthenware and bronze which fills the show-cases in the Regolini-Galassi gallery of the *Museo Gregoriano* is visible proof of this.

In the same glass-case as the chair of state stands a spherical bronze basin with dragons' heads curving inwards over the edge, giving the impression of an immense six-toed claw. A design in repoussé work beaten out from the interior is repeated round the sides four times—a fanciful group of winged oxen and winged lions—and its outlines have then been incised on the outside. Even more impressive are the two bronze cauldrons of a circumference of almost six feet, with five lions' heads on sturdy necks looking outwards, which, together with the rest of the complicated gear of their stands, were found in the ante-room. From the ante-room too came the pedestal for a cauldron, over three feet high, made of sheet bronze, which is adorned with fabulous winged creatures marching round it.

This is not the place to describe the mass of simple and of precious bronze furnishings, the platters and tureens, the fire-dogs which end in birds' heads. In the centre show-case there is the low four-wheeled 'smoke wagon'[1] enclosed by a lattice-work of sculptured lotus blossoms, with a tray for live coals over which is hung, like a bridge, the suspensory arm. This apparatus is something over forty inches in length and so far no parallel has been found outside of Etruria which might provide us with an insight into its purpose and use. It bears traces of having been used and repaired.

Another striking exhibit is a service of eleven approximately equal-sized uniformly shaped bowls of bronze from which, judging by other discoveries from this period, we may suppose a twelfth is missing. These were hung up on the side walls of the main chamber, just as was done in dwelling houses—a valuable possession displayed to view. These vessels of $8\frac{1}{2}$–$9\frac{1}{2}$ in. diameter are decorated with striking repoussé bosses in the shape of vertical ovals and bear here and there traces of having formerly been gilded. Most of them have such thin walls that we may well doubt whether they could ever have found a suitable use in everyday life. The practice of giving to the dead things made specially for the interment instead of those which could be used in everyday life, of using an earthenware copy of a helmet as cover for

[1]A kind of tray on wheels which some scholars believe may have been used for burning perfumes (translator's note).

an urn or a stone shield as substitute for a leather or bronze one over the grave pit, was already known in the Villanova time.

When we consider the abundance of the gifts and their total value, which can scarcely be ignored, as well as the costliness of this set of a dozen bowls with their thin walls and their gold plating, we can certainly exclude one theory, at least so far as the *Tomba Regolini-Galassi* and those like it are concerned, namely that the thriftiness of the survivors was the reason for making special equipment which could not, because of the quality of the materials, be used by the living. In the Beyond the dead have no longer any interest in the solidity or utility of the furnishings in the sense of the secular world, but it is desirable that they should have the object and its actual shape and that it should be offered them in a ritually correct manner. A preoccupation with the transformation ensuing on death and with the nature of the existence of spirits and souls was one of the fundamental characteristics of the Etruscans, judging by the multiplicity of their forms of burial down through the centuries. Nevertheless when studying their customs one must always bear in mind that man's nature, his feelings, emotions and impulses in relation to death often lead him, even in religious doctrines which have been philosophically perfected, to behaviour which, logically speaking, is contradictory. Indeed it is just this co-existence of things which are apparently mutually exclusive which in this context is a sign of a fullness of life.

The Shields in the Tomb

The eight great circular shields with their green patina, which, composed of numerous broken and separate pieces now reassembled, hang in the middle show-case of the right-hand side-wall of the Regolini-Galassi gallery in the Gregorian Museum, fit into the same background. They come from the ante-room in which the four-wheeled carriage also stood. Judging by the discoveries in the *Tomba degli Scudi e delle Sedie* already referred to for comparison, and many other observations pointing in the same direction right down to the gay relief-shields in the *Tomba dei Rilievi* of the second century B.C.,[1] it is permissible to assume that these shields were more than merely gorgeous decoration or a show of weapons. They served as ritual protection

[1]On the wall of the back room of the *Grotta Campana* at Veii six similar shields are painted.

for the deceased who was undergoing a transformation in the tomb, just as did the stone shields of the Villanova period. Indeed recent investigations have shown that the tomb mound itself could be regarded as a huge sacred protective shield.

These shields too are made of bronze beaten so fine that they can scarcely have been intended for use in battle. The rich ornamentation is applied in a strictly concentric design, the whole surface being filled with circular bands of different breadths, each band containing various drawings and fitting closely to the next one. Some contain purely geometrical designs, with diagonal hatching, hatched oblongs, dots and zig-zag lines. Besides these are others, richly plaited bands, a pattern of fish-scales, a frieze of animals running round, which can plainly be recognized as illustrations of the 'orientalizing' period. The close juxtaposition of old and new styles of decoration warns us not to form rigid ideas of a too strictly chronological kind in dealing with things Etruscan, for we continue to find heterogeneity even in the later years of Etruscan civilization, because these people derived such pleasure from toying with pictures and shapes which they had seen in some foreign country.

5. BUCCHERO WARE
'Bucchero Sottile' and 'Bucchero Pesante'

The varied earthenware which was found in the Regolini-Galassi tomb deserves no less attention than the bronze furnishings. Along with related ceramics from the surrounding hills it fills several of the large showcases. Three groups can be distinguished. They are typical of this period, in which the art of the East, adopted and adapted by the Hellenes, influenced the Etruscans and inspired them to assimilate and copy it as well as to create their own styles and inventions.

The first two groups comprise diverse vessels of the so-called proto-Corinthian style and local imitations of this imported ware. They confirm what the historians have already reported about the importance of the sea and Corinth's power to radiate political and intellectual influence in the seventh century B.C.

The third group consists of that gleaming deep black pottery which is known as Bucchero ware. It may be that elsewhere in the Mediterranean area at that time there was black gleaming potter's ware of fine quality, but there is no doubt that the unique technical perfection and beauty of Bucchero ware is a notable and exceptional contribution of the Etruscan masters to the cultural heritage of the ancient world. The zenith of its development lay precisely in the period of the Regolini-Galassi tomb.

Bucchero ware can be said to have its origin in the ceramics of Villanova. By this date, however, the clay was more finely sifted and washed and instead of the more or less cloudy discolorations of earlier

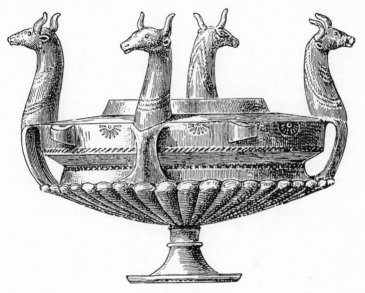

Fig. 24. Bowl from the *Tomba Calabresi* near Cerveteri, '*Bucchero sottile*' ware, first half of the seventh century B.C. Height 6⅞ in.

vessels which ranged from sandy or reddish yellow through chestnut-brown to dull black, the characteristic uniform deep black high lustre has been achieved by means of the firing technique now securely mastered. Early Bucchero ware of the period between about 680 and 600 B.C. is extraordinarily thin-walled. A sort of little wheel was used to execute the ornamentation by grooving, punching or impressing and the designs are often emphasized by whitish or ochre-coloured filling—all techniques which find a parallel in the metal-working of the same period. Alongside indigenous shapes and patterns are some copied from Corinthian examples. Many of these vessels of *Bucchero sottile* (thin-walled Bucchero ware, as this early product is called) also bear traces of having been gilded or silvered, thus showing that clay and bronze were treated alike. It must not be assumed that these Bucchero vessels of high quality were cheaper than corresponding metal vessels. We do not know for certain whether they were also used in ordinary life or were made exclusively for the dead. What has been said above about thin-walled shields and bronze bowls found in tombs will apply in this case too.

In the following period, from about 600 to 550 B.C., more use was made when decorating the still thin-walled ware of a stamping technique, which had hitherto been employed mainly in the production of larger storage vessels. This consisted in rolling off patterns from revolving seals on which were carved negative designs, some of which seem to have been imported straight from the East. They produced a relief frieze, used particularly for decorating mouths or rims of vessels. Simultaneously there emerged, at an early date, though it did not attain any particular importance before the second half of the sixth century B.C., that heavy, thick-walled pottery which is known as *Bucchero pesante*, 'heavy Bucchero ware'. It seems probable, if we can rely on the definite statements made about the places in which things were found, that the production centres up till then were in the coastal region, but that now Chiusi, situated inland, began to attain a leading position.

The persistent attachment to motives and shapes of older Corinthian pottery is noteworthy at a time when Ionic influence was asserting itself predominantly elsewhere in Etruria. This can hardly be explained simply on technical grounds such as the continued use of old models, but neither can it be explained as sheer unproductive conservatism since these elements are used quite deliberately. It seems much more likely that the Etruscans like the Greeks felt that certain styles and methods of production were indissolubly linked to specific kinds of art. Just as the hexameter of Homer remained the natural metre of the epics of Greece right down to post-classical times, and underwent only slight adaptations, and just as in Hellas the technique of shading in painting and drawing, for example, was never during long centuries used when representing the female body; so the old Corinthian shapes and illustrations belong to Bucchero ware from its beginning right down to its gradual disappearance in the first decades of the fifth century B.C.

The Potter's Technique

In the production of heavy ware the potter goes about the first stages of his work in a manner no different from the bronze-founder. He creates a solid sculptured model out of some perishable workable material, such as wax or pitch. This he clothes in a coating of clay which is then hardened in a furnace, while at the same time the effect of the heat melts the plastic core. The mould thus produced he places on the potter's wheel, clothing it in Bucchero clay prepared for this purpose, kneading and moulding it; then he hollows it out evenly and with the usual potter's technique evolves a foot and a neck and a mouth or opening. Handles and additional plastic decoration, above all human heads, animal *protomes* and entwining snakes, are formed separately and attached. Finally there follows, as in the case of bronze castings, an overall finishing process in the course of which any casting burrs or seams and unevennesses are smoothed away, interior drawings are added by engraving, and polishing is carried out. Fingerprints and signs of turning operations traceable on individual vessels have made it possible to establish that this was the procedure and so to confirm that from the technical angle there is a close connexion between Bucchero ware and metal work.

It is essential to bear clearly in mind the fact that Etruscan pictorial skill, even when it shows a trend towards Greek shapes and designs, starts out from material which, in bronze casting as in pottery and even in stone-work, is soft and malleable, and which positively tempts one to improvise and to give rein to fantasy. The Etruscans never used the crystalline, light-demanding marble of the Hellenes as a working material or as an object of artistic analysis, any more than they used the heavy resistant basalt or porphyry of the Egyptians. They sought rather the challenge which lay in the tractability of a material and in its capacity for transformation which, as it were, drove them to create one form after another out of it.

Spontaneity and Conservativism

A delight in transposing separate elements of a shape, in conferring individuality by light finishing touches on models turned out of a mould and in permitting something unexpected to spring forth spontaneously from the touch of sensitive hands is expressed in many works of the Etruscans. Wax and clay, therefore, remained for them basic materials and gold of course fascinated them. Tuff, from which they created their large-scale sculptures, when they were not using a sandy limestone,—*pietra fetida*—terracotta or bronze for the purpose, was, when fresh cut, like raw, uniformly dense earth, another sort of clay if you will, which only became hard when it had been exposed to the air for a considerable time. Alabaster, which was used increasingly in the later period, particularly for the production of urns decorated with reliefs, was a sort of soft malleable precious gypsum, which could, with the aid of oil and wood, be given a softly reflecting brilliance. As it could be made to resemble marble, it was used wherever, as in Volterra during the second and first centuries B.C., there was any question of emulating the works produced in marble by Hellenistic sculptors.

From the beginning of the seventh century B.C. onwards there can be observed, in Greek art, the action of a will growing visibly stronger, which aims at mastering and controlling the powers and forces of the underworld by the creation of shapes durable as crystal and of laws universally valid. When the artist, as in the hall of the Core (maidens)[1] in the Erechtheum in Athens, realizes in human form the forces which can bear a weight by virtue of being held together under tension in a pillar and represents them as maidens carrying baskets beneath the rigid beams, this is an exception and an event, and the beam-supports in their turn are transformed into architecture and become an integral part of the structure. This is a feature of Greek art at its best.

To the Etruscan on the other hand form as such has in general little meaning. Unconcernedly, indeed instinctively he dismisses portraits and faces from the walls of his vessels and the decoration of his furniture. A mere hook shoots forth tendrils and blossoms, turns into a bird's neck or a twining snake. From the jaw of a lion grows the handle of a jug, which rises to divide and encircle the mouth of the jug as a pair of snakes. A can turns into a miraculous bird with the bearded head of a man or gazes out of enormous lashless eyes carved right and left of the spout under the cloverleaf-shaped opening. The body of the vessel is a sculptured head with nose and mouth and long side-whiskers framing the round face. Men's and animals' bodies are elongated like plasticine figures or are shrunk into themselves; pointing hands are disproportionately large. Three dimensional art is interpenetrated and complemented without inhibition by art in two dimensions. Expression and

[1] i.e. porch of the Caryatides (translator's note).

pre-eminence are given to a world which we would probably describe as animistic because it recognized that every thing and every being is mysteriously possessed of a daemonic soul, and which makes us think rather of the surging abundance of the *numina* in the religion of the Romans than of Greece.

Yet Hellas too was capable of such creations. In the art of the orientalizing period (also called the Idaean period) they burst out of the bonds in which the geometric style had held them. It is only through the numerous archaeological discoveries and studies of recent decades that this non-classical art has become plainer and known far beyond the restricted world of the specialists, particularly through the bronze shields from the cave of Zeus on Mount Ida, the bronze furnishings and fittings from Olympia and the early Attic ceramics from the Cerameicus of Athens. Research work on Homer, following these discoveries, has shown the degree to which the 'Odyssey' in particular drew pictorial force from this revolution.

The *Bucchero pesante* of the Etruscans has not only many formal links with old Corinthian ware, but was also influenced in its basic features by experiences and opinions to which Hellas was addicted in the very decades when Etruria came into decisive contact with her. The heavy black utensils with their multiple possibilities and with their world of shapes filled with faces and daemonies, reveal that forces and attitudes still held sway in Etruria at the beginning of the fifth century B.C. which in Greece had gone out of use long before and had practically sunk into oblivion. From this it is plain that Etruria was not under the influence of Greece—which was so decisive for her—in the classical period of Hellas but in the colonization era when revolution and upheavals had already deeply affected the religion and social organization of Hellas. It was by coming to terms with this experience that Etruria created her own character and acquired her individuality.

6. GOLD WORK

The Art of Granulation

Gold has always exercised a mysterious magic on mankind. Etruscan jewellery, however, is capable of spellbinding the modern spectator in a special way. Visitors crowd in front of the jewellery show-cases in museums and exhibitions. The discoveries in one single tomb such as the admittedly somewhat exceptional *Tomba Regolini-Galassi* are sufficient to give us an impression of the riches which abounded among the leading families at the time when Etruria came into contact with the Mediterranean trade, of the value then attached to artistically worked gold and of the marvellous skill which their handworkers speedily acquired.

As with ceramics, there are typical imported items alongside native work among the worked metal items from the Regolini-Galassi tomb, an indication of the variety of Etruria's foreign connexions even in early times. The gilded hemispherical silver bowls with rich pictorial decoration, incised and repoussé rows of warriors and lions, palm trees and processions of riders, point to Egypt and Cyprus. The six classically beautiful silver goblets with the name of their owner, Larthia (Fig. 25), come from some Greek workshop on the spot or abroad or at the very least are copied from the proto-Corinthian *skyphos* which was widely popular.

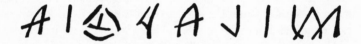

Fig. 25. Inscription on a small silver vessel from the Regolini–Galassi tomb near Cerveteri, first half of the seventh century B.C.

But the most remarkable of the small items from the Regolini-Galassi tomb on display are the pieces of jewellery decorated with granulation, in particular a pair of broad armlets with a picture of a feminine trinity repeated several times round them[1] and the great disc *fibula* with the lion shield.[2] The technique of granulation did not itself originate in Etruria. It had a long history in the East. Tiny little gold balls are fixed on to the main body of the gold ornament in such a way that they form lines or, as in the silhouette style of the Vetulonian masters, fill in particular flat spaces. Moreover the Etruscan artists knew so well how to join these little balls to the background and to one another that they neither sank into it nor were melted away, but are revealed to the eye on closer examination as each forming an independent creation throwing its own shadow. From the side one can see

[1]Inv. No. 668. Diam. 4 in., width 2¾ in.
[2]Inv. No. 669. Height 12⅜ in., width 9 in.–9½ in.

between the little balls although their diameter is only a few hundredths of an inch.

Goldsmiths who have striven to recapture this lost technique know what skill was needed to achieve such junctions. For on account of the

Fig. 26. Ornamental gold pin with granulation, from Vetulonia, second half of the seventh century B.C., 7⅝ in. long

large superficial area exposed to radiation, these little balls, consisting of the same material as their background, start to melt when they are heated, while the ground to which they are to be joined without losing their shape still remains absolutely firm.

The things which took place in smoke and soot during this process must have appeared puzzling and dangerous to a world as yet a stranger to scientific thinking, which still measured its discoveries against experiences of the soul and mythical descriptions. The actual production of the little balls was itself a kind of magic. Little pieces are snipped off bundles of finest gold wire and fall without touching each other into a crucible filled with coal dust. The crucible is heated to a high temperature and when the dust has once grown cold and is rinsed out it is seen that the little pieces of wire have melted into uniform-sized little balls. These have then to be amalgamated in a special way with copper salts and joined to the background which they are to adorn by means of saliva or fish glue, or some other sticky substance which will be partially transformed into carbon in the ensuing melting process. The final junction is then ultimately achieved, by means of carefully directed heat, as a chemical process. The whole proceeding is accompanied by a play of changing colours created by the sparks and flames. It is easy to understand the aura of respect and fear which surrounded those who had the power to do such things and which led them to live a life apart within society, and it is easy to see why the Etruscans included Sethlans (Vulcan), the smiths' god, in the number of the great gods who had power over lightning.

Granulation and Nailing

Granulation, which here attains a high degree of perfection, is basically related to the ornamental use of nail heads and rivets. The two techniques are found side by side at a very early date in the ancient East, and were both used for the same purpose. The heads of metal nails, originally used to unite parts which had been manufactured separately, such as the hilt of the sword with the sword, acquire an independent existence when detached from their intrinsic purpose. For the Etruscans of the end of the eighth and beginning of the seventh century B.C. too, nail heads play a certain role as decoration alongside granulation, which was used for gold jewellery and only for that. They are found particularly on earthenware urns and urn-helmets and on objects made of wood.[1]

It is not difficult to fit into the context of the art of the smith, of

[1] Perhaps the ancient Eastern custom of decorating walls with a pattern of gaily coloured clay-nails set closely together has the same origin.

granulation and nailing, the story of the 'year nail' which was annually driven into the wall of the temple of the goddess of destiny at Volsinii (cf. p. 12). But the meagre data which we possess are as in so many other instances inadequate for the tracing of an absolutely reliable connexion. What took place in Volsinii was indeed the filling of a predetermined space with nails, but the object of the exercise was not primarily to produce a wall-decoration in the shrine but to outlaw the past and reveal destiny fulfilling itself irresistibly and driving on to a fixed end. We do not know what other ideas of a special nature may possibly also be associated with granulation. Another method of working, less subtle but scarcely more recent, which also developed from ornamental nailing, is that in which bosses punched from the reverse side are used instead of the little gold beads, a technique which, admittedly coarser, had already appeared on the bronze helmets of the later Villanova culture.

7. SIGNS OF RANK

The Golden Pectoral

A most pressing question is that of the rank, importance, and destiny of Larthia, buried in the Regolini-Galassi tomb. The marks of ownership borne by her silverware provide nothing more than the name, and give no indication whatsoever of her origin and family. History tells of no woman of this name, and the sparse notes scattered here and there in the annals of Cerveteri make no mention of the exploits of any princess. She lies lonely in her mausoleum. For the man buried in the antechamber can scarcely, in view of the usual customs of Cerveteri, have been her husband, since otherwise he would have been laid in the same place. Or did the dead woman in her lifetime possess a rank which elevated her so far above all others, even her own spouse, that she had to lie alone in her tomb?

Like the dead woman in the Bocchoris tomb near Tarquinii, she wore a robe heavily embroidered with artistically worked gold, the details of which we can unfortunately no longer discern with any certainty. The visitor stands fascinated in front of the necklace with the pendants of amber set in gold, and the gold spirals which fastened her curls, the buckle of her belt, the *fibulae* and armlets, the earrings, and the lotus blossoms which were fixed to her shoes as gold ornaments.

Dominating everything among these items lies a piece of gold foil

Fig. 27. Gold pectoral from the Regolini-Galassi tomb near Cerveteri, first half of the seventh century B.C. Height 16½ in.

16½ in. long and almost as broad, in the shape of a large pectoral or 'bib' which was probably worn as such[1] (Fig. 27). It was originally slightly convex and backed with sheet copper, ample traces of which were still to be seen when it was first discovered. The surface is covered from the outside edge to the middle by narrow bands running parallel to the edge, which in their turn are filled completely with rows of ornamentation in the orientalizing style. Lines of little bosses punched

[1]Inv. No. 695. 15 in. × 16½ in.

close to one another, making an effect of beads, separate the bands from each other.

Similar pieces for comparison are rare, though they have been found in Tarquinii, Marsigliana d'Albegna and Rome. It is clear that we are dealing here with a symbol of rank reserved for only a few privileged persons and that its use was restricted to a relatively short period of time. One could probably claim that the breast-plates of the small Sardinian bronzes were their precursors. But with something which appears for such a short period and points so unequivocally to connexions with the East as this does, one can most probably get nearer to its significance by examining the artistic and traditional wares of the Near East.

On a bronze bowl from Nimrud in the British Museum in London a winged sphinx runs victoriously triumphant in front of the swiftly travelling hunting chariot of the king. The sphinx is wearing a 'bib' which in shape and size is very similar to that worn by the dead woman in the Regolini-Galassi tomb.

Even more directly comparable is the golden breast-plate of the valuable amber statuette now in the Museum of Fine Arts in Boston which depicts the Assyrian King Ashur-nasir-pal II (883–59 B.C.) as a royal priest.[1] The 'bib', divided horizontally, is in this case decorated with nine rosettes in so many panels, each divided regularly into three and three. Finally the description in Exodus, Chapter 28, of the similar breast-plate which Moses had made for Aaron as the 'breast-plate of judgment' on the instructions of Jahwe (Jehovah), shows that these panels and rosettes probably had a specific meaning:—

'And thou shalt make the breast-plate of judgment with cunning work; after the work of the ephod thou shalt make it; of gold, of blue, and of purple, and of scarlet and of fine twined linen, shalt thou make it. Foursquare it shall be being doubled; a span shall be the length thereof, and a span shall be the breadth thereof. And thou shalt set in it settings of stones, even four rows of stone. . . . And the stones shall be with the names of the children of Israel. . . . And Aaron shall bear the names of the children of Israel in the breast-plate of judgment upon his heart, when he goeth in unto the holy place, for a memorial before the Lord continually.'

Thus these gold plates covering the breast have their place in the

[1] Inv. No. 38. 1936, height 9⅝ in., allegedly from Kalchu, ninth century B.C.

series of jewels from which emanated religious power and the splendour
of authority in the same way as the golden fleece and the shield of
Athena of mythology. For the significance of the ornamentation on
the Etruscan example, however, we possess no key.

The Disc Fibula with the Lion Decoration

The second large piece among the gold items from the Regolini-
Galassi tomb seems to point in the same direction. This is the magnificent disc *fibula* with the lion shield already mentioned (Fig. 28). Its
full height is almost 12½ in. i.e. a good 50 per cent more than that other
somewhat older piece which can be compared with it on the basis of
style or ornamentation, the piece which came from Vulci and is now
to be found in the Munich '*Museum für antike Kleinkunst*'.[1] That there
is a link with the usual Italic disc fibula is undisputed but we have before
us here a peculiar form obviously designed for a special purpose, as is
proved by the two detached semi-cylindrical shaped cross-pieces,
linked to one another by a hinge and decorated at the ends with pendants in the shape of palm leaves. It is not easy to find any technical
explanation for these long cross-pieces which are absent from the
standard type of *fibula*.

The pin of the brooch is fixed under a convex plate of gold just over
four inches long and almost equally wide, the protective hood of the
pin beneath a circular shield of double the size, the centre of which is
filled with five lions passant beaten out of sheet gold. They are en-
circled by two bands separated from each other by a smooth strip, each
with a pattern of symmetrically intertwining flowers. An imaginative
interpreter has seen this smooth strip as a river bordered by overgrown
banks. The smaller shield, shaped like the leaf of a lime tree, is adorned
with seven rows of plastically depicted ducks facing upwards, between
which, in corresponding rows, are lions beaten lightly out of the background.

All this elaborate and artistic repoussé work is enhanced and sub-
tilized by the finest granulation wherever there is room for it. The
outlines of the lions and the blossoms, the fine zigzag pattern which
covers the two detached cross-bars and the fifty-five ducks are each a
small work of art in themselves and nowhere does the work of the
master, so sure of his technique in every respect, become slipshod. Yet

[1]Museum of Small Works of Antique Art.

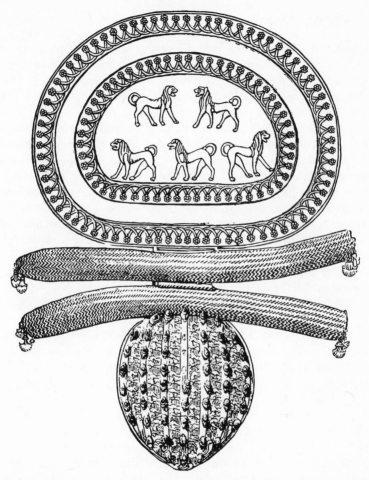

Fig. 28. Gold disc fibula (clasp) from the Regolini-Galassi tomb near Cerveteri, first half of the seventh century B.C.

despite the wealth of detail the overall effect is preserved and the eye is drawn to the lustrous and clearly designed lion disc.

Unfortunately we cannot now with certainty determine how this valuable showpiece was worn. It is evident that the lion disc was at the top and thus that the pin was inserted from below upwards, and equally that the hinge in the middle made it easier to grip masses of fabric than if the whole thing had been completely rigid as it is now after its restoration. From reports of later discoveries, admittedly not entirely acceptable, there is some probability that this may have been an ornament on a headdress affixed above the forehead. Reliable analogies for such a contrivance have not hitherto been established in Etruria. One is tempted to think of the crowns of the Egyptian gods and Pharaohs.

Though shape and technique make it obvious that this is native Etruscan work, yet the style of the art and the figures themselves have such an oriental flavour that we cannot reject as impossible the theory that this pin was used for a purpose which can not yet be proved to have existed in later Etruria. The golden breast-plate also had no permanent significance. On Syrian bowls such as those found in the *Tomba Regolini-Galassi* itself and in Praeneste there are illustrations of the goddess Isis wearing over her forehead a winged disc of the sun. Even though there has not so far been found in Italy any direct proof of the existence of such head ornaments we may yet reckon with the possibility that they did exist as ceremonial adornments.

The lions and the water birds suggest the same 'Great Mistress' who is portrayed on the broad armlets of Larthia along with the old oriental lion-killer Gilgamesh as 'Mistress of the Beasts'. Is it possible that the dead lady was distinguished by the peculiar head ornament and the golden breast-plate as 'Divine Mistress'? Was she able to wear these emblems even in her lifetime perhaps on certain solemn occasions just as the 'Victor' in Rome was allocated in accordance with a custom proved to be Etruscan the dress and the vehicle of Tinia, because he was, for the period of the triumph, not only a religious symbol but in truth the heavenly god himself moving visibly among men?

We do not know and can only guess that mysterious and high honours were connected with the golden jewellery. Once again we are reminded of the tradition already mentioned (p. 26) that the Etruscans possessed the secret skill to make their dead become immortal gods, *Di manales*.

Plate XIII.

Bucchero statues dating from the seventh century B.C.

(By courtesy of Kohlhammer Verlag, Stuttgart)

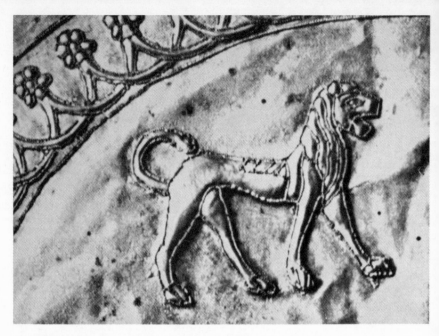

Plate XIV (a). Detail of golden clasp shown in Fig. 28 (*Vatican Museum*)

Plate XIV (b). A Golden bowl (*Victoria and Albert Museum*)

CHAPTER V

The Conflict with the Greeks

I. DEMARATUS OF CORINTH

THE first time we come across the Etruscans mentioned by name in Greek literature is about the year 700 B.C.[1] How many Hellenic seafarers' experiences of Etruria had already gone into the 'Odyssey' cannot be determined in detail. But Hesiod, in the last lines of his 'Theogony', names as kings 'of all the far-renowned Tyrsenians' Agrius and Latinus 'the faultless and powerful', the two sons whom Circe, daughter of the sun-god, bore to Ulysses. It is plain that Latins and Tyrrhenians are not in his eyes to be distinguished from one another. In fact the discoveries in the great mound-tombs of the orientalizing period do show such a close intellectual and cultural union between southern Etruria and Latium that it seems easier to accept that there was a frontier between them and the northern part of Tuscany than that there was any division of the peoples right and left of the lower Tiber. This fellowship appears repeatedly in the following period despite the growing evidence of independence in the individual city-states and it is rather remarkable to see it still in operation in the Middle Ages and in the Renaissance, indeed right up to recent times, in the state of tension between Florence and Rome.

And so the description, which sounds like a legend, of the origin in Hellas of the royal family of the Tarquins leads us into the middle of the seventh century B.C. For it is related that in the year 657 B.C. when the oligarchical rule of the Bacchiades in Corinth was overthrown by Cypselus, the leader of the Demos, a certain Demaratus, hitherto one of

[1]We need not at this point take into account something which does not directly affect the history of Italo-Etruscan culture, namely the much discussed problem of the possible connexion between the 'Tr̝sa', mentioned in Egyptian inscriptions of the thirteenth century B.C., during the 'Time of the Great Migration', and the Tyrrhenians; nor the occurrence of the name of the Tyrsenians in conjunction with the Pelasgians in the Eastern Mediterranean area.

the ruling class, fled, and at the end of his flight finally came to Tarquinii. He was received with hospitality and married into one of the leading families. He had two sons who bore the Etruscan rulers' names of Lucumo and Aruns. One of these, Lucumo, won the celebrated Tanaquil as wife. She later prevailed on him to emigrate to Rome and helped him to become king and ruler there. It is said that the Etruscans learned writing and painting and also the plastic arts from Demaratus personally and the Corinthian masters belonging to his retinue.[1]

Chronologically the lapse of time between the seizing of power by Cypselus and the time when, according to the Roman table of kings, the first Tarquinius reigned in Rome is so great that it must be questioned whether we have not here two originally independent accounts which have been amalgamated at a later date to create a King-myth. The names handed down for the artists—Eucheir and Eugrammos, 'Dexterous' and 'Fine Draughtsman'—sound like the names of the sons of Klopfstock the schoolmaster 'Pinkepank' and 'Piffpaff'[2] though of course that does not prove that they are invented. It still remains most probable that the Tuscan alphabet comes from Cumae (cf. p. 35), certainly not from Corinth. Moreover, contact with that Hellenic city on the isthmus, ruler of the sea, is, as discoveries of Corinthian ceramics prove, considerably older than this legend would make it. But, despite these reservations, the Demaratus story does acquire the weight of a historical document, when viewed as a whole against the background of the powerful influence of Corinth on Etruscan culture.

It is scarcely possible to determine with any more certainty whether the Greek heroes named in legends of the founding of Etruscan cities denote a memory of an immigration from this or that region of Hellas and possess a historical background, or whether they were only brought into the picture to fit in with later speculations. But we would do well not to forget that according to the evidence of pottery discoveries it was not only from Corinth that Greek influence reached Etruria. The Hellenic cities of lower Italy and of Sicily are also stamped with the impression of the artistic achievement of the Corinthians with whom

[1] Of importance is the suggestion that there was a genealogical link between Hercules and the Bacchiades and the Tarquins, particularly as the Hercules myth was later used elsewhere to prove a genealogical link between the Tyrsenians and the Mysians (see also p. 30).

[2] In the fairy tale by Clemens von Brentano called '*Das Märchen von dem Schulmeister Klopfstock und seinen fünf Söhnen*' (translator's note).

they maintained active connexions. But mention of Cumae and its significance for the origin of the Etruscan alphabet is sufficient to indicate how much remains hidden from us—despite all the efforts of archaeologists—when written sources are lacking.

Thus we can trace feeble, if positive signs of the strong impulses which emanated from Crete particularly in the second half of the seventh century B.C. not only in the direction of Hellas, but clearly also towards Etruria. The earliest large-scale sculpture in Etruria, the puzzling fragments of sculptured stone in the Vetulonia cupola-tomb known as the Pietrera, do perhaps suggest a link between them and Corinth via the pediment decoration of the temple of Artemis on Corcyra,[1] but the early tomb-sculptures of Vulci—the centaur and the rider on the seahorse, carved out of the grey volcanic nenfro—point to more direct contacts with the island of Minos, as do also the shape and layout of certain cupola-tombs of Populonia.

2. THE BATTLE WITH THE PHOCAEANS
Herodotus' Account

The first event in Etruscan history of which ancient historians have given us fairly precise information is the naval battle which was fought in Sardinian waters between the Phocaeans (Greeks from the coast of Asia Minor) on the one side and the combined Carthaginians and Etruscans on the other. It is true that Thucydides reports only briefly that the Phocaeans, who founded Massilia, the Marseilles of to-day, defeated the Carthaginians at sea. Herodotus however gives a much more detailed description of the events of that day.

The Phocaeans had had to retreat before the Persians out of their city-state which was situated not far from Smyrna. Their attempt to settle on the archipelago of the Oenussae, some thirty miles off the shore of their homeland, was wrecked by the resistance of the inhabitants of Chios, who feared commercial competition and therefore refused to sell the islands. These people, the first of the Hellenes, it is said, to have made long sea voyages, were already long accustomed to press with their fifty-oared battleships into the Adriatic, into the Tyrrhenian Sea, and indeed even as far as Tartessus in Spain. They now sailed and rowed, with wives and children and all movable property, towards the west and ultimately made landfall in Corsica. Twenty years before,

[1]Corfu (translator's note).

Phocaean emigrants, in pursuance of the not absolutely clear utterance of some oracle, had founded the city of Alalia there on the coast facing Italy, and, says Herodotus, the newcomers 'lived for five years alongside those who had come hither earlier, built temples and practised piracy against all their neighbours.'

At length the Carthaginians and the Etruscans undertook a combined operation against the troublesome intruders. Each contributed sixty ships so that they went against the sixty longboats of the Phocaeans with twice the numbers. Nonetheless the latter were the victors. However, they lost two-thirds of their sea power and the remaining ships were so damaged that they were no longer serviceable.[1] Thus the Phocaeans had to give up Corsica. They embarked their wives and children and whatever else the damaged fleet could carry, and journeyed first to Rhegium at the southern tip of Italy, then again farther north, until they succeeded at last in coming to rest in Hyele, which the Romans called Velia, south of Paestum, which later became famous as the seat of the Eleatic school of philosophy, to which it gave its name. It is not recorded whether they founded Marseilles before or after this sea battle.

The crews of the Phocaean ships which were rammed and became incapable of manoeuvring in the battle fell for the most part into the hands of the combined Carthaginians and Etruscans. They were brought to land and most of them were stoned to death. It is clear that this occurred in the vicinity of Cerveteri or Agylla as the Greeks called it; for Herodotus reports further how all the inhabitants, indeed even the cattle and the sheep of this city, when they passed by this place of ill-fame were suddenly overcome by symptoms of paralysis, sprains and crippling. Emissaries were dispatched to Delphi to obtain advice from the Apollo of the Hellenes, and in Cerveteri a hundred years later propitiation ceremonies were still taking place regularly with horse-racing and competitive sports, as the Pythoness had directed.

[1]According to Herodotus, I, 166, 2, the twenty seaworthy Phocaean ships which survived were unserviceable because they had lost their 'beaks' (prows made for ramming). F. Miltner, in his book *Über die Herkunft der etruskischen Schiffe*, p. 113 *et seq. esp.* pp. 116/7, finds in this remark confirmation of his hypothesis, based mainly on pictorial evidence, that the Etruscans on this occasion and indeed in general used especially heavily built sailing ships, of a type to which he believes one can see parallels in the *Camara* known to have been in the eastern Black Sea during the time of the Roman emperors, and in the later Byzantine *Dromone*.

The Battle with the Phocaeans

No Etruscan Sea Power

Despite its pronounced Greek bias this report does throw a strong and significant light on the situation in Etruria during the second half of the sixth century B.C. Objects excavated and written sources alike point to a peak having been reached in Etruscan evolution. Great wealth fills the tombs, the arts flourish and on the throne of Rome are kings who come from Tarquinii. Yet even then the Tyrsenians clearly do not in general figure as a sea power properly speaking.

The Greeks are able to establish themselves unhindered opposite the Etruscan coast and from there, for twenty years with relatively weak forces, then for a further five years strengthened by their fellow countrymen driven out of their own homes by the Persians, they ravage the Tyrsenian shore and practise piracy. About the same time the sage Bias of Priene is advising all the hard-pressed Ionians of Asia Minor to unite in one body, set sail for Sardinia, there found a city, and lead a life of comfort and freedom as masters over other peoples. There is no hint of an Etruscan sea power which might hinder such plans, although relics of pottery and sculpture prove that there existed at that time a lively traffic between both regions of the Mediterranean.

Obviously the twelve great rich cities of the Etruscan Confederation possessed no common fleet strong enough to go to meet the men of the newly founded Phocaean settlement on Corsica in spite of the fact that at least Cerveteri, Tarquinii, Vetulonia and Populonia were after all maritime cities. In Herodotus' account Agylla-Cerveteri is actually the only one mentioned, and the number of ships attributed to the Etruscans (i.e. sixty) is not so large that they came necessarily from several city-states. The Phocaeans alone had as many (and what is more, obviously larger and more battleworthy) ships to throw in and the Carthaginians took part in the battle with a like number.

So once again it is confirmed that the Etruscan Confederation was not a military power. Nothing leads us to suppose that this was anything more than an operation undertaken jointly by the Carthaginians and the Agyllaeans. Like the cities of Greece each Etruscan city was autonomous despite the existence of common religious centres and festivals. In Hellas the period of politico-military unions of the type of the Attic-Delian maritime league begins only in the fifth century B.C. and there is no clear evidence that Etruria anticipated this development or even imitated it.

There is also no sign that the naval battle near Sardinia was a dispute between the Etruscans and the Greeks as such over a matter of principle, or one based on blood relationships or nationalism. On the contrary, Herodotus' report makes it plain that this is an encounter, so to speak, within the framework of the ancient world, which is scarcely to be rated differently from the naval battle described by Thucydides as the first Greek encounter at sea, between Corinth and its colony, the city of Corcyra, or any other clash between neighbours. It is true that the Phocaean prisoners were stoned to death, but the slaughter of prisoners of war or of at least some of them can be seen as a lapse into ancient customs like the sacrifice of the captured Trojan youths in Homer.

Slaughter of Prisoners

In the year 355 B.C. the Tarquinians slaughtered three hundred and seven captured Romans as sacrifices, for which they were however to pay just as dearly four years later. Three hundred and fifty-eight noble Tarquinians, who in their turn had fallen into captivity, were beaten with rods on the market place in Rome as revenge and then beheaded, all those who were taken prisoner with them being slain on the spot where the battle took place. With gruesome realism tomb-paintings in the *Tomba François* at Vulci, which dates from near the end of the same century, depict the butchering of the twelve young Trojans by Achilles at the funeral of Patroclus and the reliefs on limestone and alabaster urns of later date frequently utilize this and similar subjects of Greek legend.

The old Italic custom of human sacrifice at the tomb survives almost undisguised till deep into historical times in the form of gladiatorial contests which the Romans introduced in the year 264 B.C. from the Campania (long governed by Tyrrhenians) and which they continued to carry on in the manner learned there. On these occasions those who were killed were dragged away by a man disguised in Etruscan fashion as a demon of the underworld, the Dispater, who was equipped with a large mallet and sharp-pointed horses' ears and a hideous mask (see Figs. 29 and 34). As late as the funeral ceremonies in honour of the father and uncle of Scipio the Younger in Spain such life and death contests took place, in which those who fought were not slaves but free men. We have evidence from tomb-paintings in the *Tomba degli Auguri* of bloody masked games of this kind taking place in Tarquinii precisely at the

Fig. 29. Demon of death, tomb painting, early fourth century B.C.

period of the Agyllaean stoning of the Phocaeans. They were in those days an integral part of the funeral ceremonies and only later became a popular form of entertainment without symbolic significance.

The dead need the 'special juice' of blood to give them strength. Certainly the practice of offering human sacrifices appears to have been suppressed relatively early in Hellas and elsewhere and replaced by offerings of animals. Yet, in a country like Etruria where spiritual life was governed by and subservient to the powers of the unknown, natural and spontaneous feelings of revulsion or horror, which might have resisted the cold-blooded slaughter of human beings to comply with some religious dogma, were comparatively weak and easily swept aside in obedience to some imaginative impulse. So the crime of the victorious inhabitants of Cerveteri is seen to be not the actual slaying of the Phocaean ships' crews: their offence is rather that in an access of wild hatred they stoned the men who had fallen into their hands, pirates who had for years impeded their voyages, caused distress to their wives and children and plundered the coast. By their unbridled frenzy they have deprived the gods and likewise their own dead of what was due to them and only given rein to their own wrath. In revenge they suffer exactly the misfortunes they inflicted on the Greeks —sprains, crippling and paralysis, which had their origin in the place where the stoning took place.[1]

It is significant that in their trouble the Etruscans of Agylla turn not to any indigenous oracle or to their own priests and *haruspices*, but to the Apollo of Delphi. The link with Hellas remains so natural and un-questioned, in spite of what had happened, that the Pythoness gives advice and a reply as a matter of course and exactly as she would have if a Hellenic city had put the question. Without reservation Cerveteri accepts what the Delphic sibyl imposes and does not in the years to come cease from organizing these regular contests regardless of the state of relationships with different individual Greek states at any given time. From various finds we learn that the slaughter of the Phocaeans did not weaken the contact with Hellas in Cerveteri or anywhere else in Etruria. Indeed Ionic products at that period had such a very strong influence on Etruscan art, that an era of Ionic-Attic influence has actu-ally been spoken of. In Cerveteri itself there was at that very time a pottery workshop which was in all probability conducted by an Ionian, the master who created the 'Caeretan Hydria', the water jar so gay and rich in invention which takes its name from the town. Among the

[1]Cf. Virgil, 'Aeneid' VI, 358–62 and 378–81: The inhabitants of the Italic coast assaulted the shipwrecked helmsman Palinurus as he struggled to land. 'They took me erroneously to be a prize. Now the tide and the winds drive me relentlessly to the shore.' To the dying man's agonized cries the soothsayer replies in the same terms as might have been used to the Phocaeans when they were being stoned to death: 'Far and wide in the cities the neighbouring peoples shall be terrified by portents from the heavens and to make atonement to thy bones they shall erect a mound to thee and offer sacrifices at the mound; and the place shall bear forever thy name Palinurus.'

treasure chests of the Greek cities in the shrine of Apollo at Delphi there stood one single Etruscan one and it belonged to the Agyllaeans.

3. THE MONARCHY

The Tarquins Expelled from Rome

It is difficult to tell whether the year 510/509 B.C. played an important role in the history of the Etruscans as well as of the Romans, for whom it meant the end of a rule by kings which had deteriorated into

Fig. 30. Tomb painting, about 520 B.C.

tyranny and the beginning of their republican government. Yet one would be doing wrong to the legendary accounts if one regarded the expulsion of Tarquinius Superbus as a revolt against the predominance of Tarquinii and the abolition of the monarchy as a blow against Etruscanism as such. There is no proof that Rome had hitherto been a satellite of Tarquinii as had the city-domain of Cerveteri, and nothing to prove that she ever belonged to the Confederation of the Twelve in any way. Indeed the fact that Rome did not belong to the Etruscan Amphictyonic League centred on the sacred Voltumna grove of Volsinii and did belong to the Latin Confederation grouped around the mountain shrine of Jupiter on Mons Albanus, Monte Cavo above Rocca di Papa in the Alban hills, may perhaps be a decisive reason for the growing independence which Rome was developing *vis-à-vis* Etruria. The wisdom of the *haruspices* was listened to and their counsel followed, but life and thought were not governed by the Tagetic doctrine. The cultural connexion between southern Etruria and Latium was maintained for a long time to come, regardless of political developments.

The royal power of the Tarquins was not necessarily anything more than what legend reports, namely the rule of a family of Etrusco-Greek origin, immigrants in Rome, which was from time to time interrupted.

Fig. 31. Tomb painting, about 520 B.C.

It has very properly been pointed out that one peculiarity of the Roman kings in comparison with those of the Etruscans was that the individual rulers did not reign as offspring of an ancient royal family or by virtue of their royal blood, but as individuals who had come to this power by destiny or skill and also that Servius, son of a virgin, and not a blood relative, came between the first of the Tarquins and his profligate son in the succession.

So it is that even after the expulsion of Superbus one single powerful individual seeks to bring under his rule the Roman state, weakened through rebellion and the intrigues of the expelled Tarquin. This is Porsenna, subject of so many legends, sometimes celebrated as king of Chiusi or of Volsinii, sometimes as Lord over all Etruria, who still cannot be placed definitely in a historical setting. There is much evidence that he may for a period have succeeded to some extent in his ambition. But what is really decisive is that never again does one man alone exercise permanent power, whosoever he may be or whatsoever his origin. The time for that has expired, the citizens are no longer ready to tolerate it.

It is no accident that in the annals of Rome the year of the expulsion of the last Tarquin coincides with that of the expulsion of the last tyrant from Athens, namely Hippias, the son of Pisistratus, and that Tarquinius Superbus himself is portrayed in the same colours as the Greek tyrants. Central Italy, Etruscan and Latin alike, is so closely linked to Hellas that she not only takes note of the social and political upheavals taking place there, but allows herself to be directly influenced by them. It is not only Rome which throws off the rule of kings—the same process begins to take place in the Etruscan cities although it is true that the information we possess about them is lacking in detail.

Priest-Kings

Anyone who studies the social history of Rome, boiling in an almost perpetual state of unpredictable upheaval, and the relatively definite picture of other states of ancient times, must be painfully aware how little we know in this particular respect about the Etruscans. This lack of knowledge cannot be compensated for by analyses, however meticulous, of archaeological discoveries.

It is clear that originally kings ruled over the separate city-states. They were probably called *lucumones*—in Etruscan *lauchme, luchume*. The Romans traced back to them the insignia of office of their highest officials—the golden crown (*corona aurea*) and the purple-embroidered state robe (*trabea*), the symbols of honour (*phalerae*), the throne of state (*sella curulis*), the ring of office (*annulus*) and the bundle of rods (*fasces*).

Above all, however, the 'triumph' of the victorious general and the dress usual for that ceremony, were alleged to go back to the *lucumones* via the Tarquins. From these allegations and certain data in the old Roman calendar of festivals, it emerges that these *lucumones* were by their very nature originally priest-kings. Like the Roman 'victor' later, the *lucumones* had to wear the cloak of heaven embroidered with stars and like him colour their faces with vermilion, ride in on a chariot drawn by white horses, and, by virtue of their kingship, actually become for the time being Tinia, the god of the heavens himself, made visible and active among human beings. The sceptre crowned by an eagle was theirs by right. Their activities were originally linked to the phases of the moon and the passing of the year. Time was measured by their sacrificial acts and their announcements of festivals in harmony with events in the heavens. At each quarter of the moon the *lucumo* showed himself in a solemn ceremony to the people to permit them to salute him and do him honour, to offer sacrifices, and to discover what was the will of the divine powers and what was destined to happen. He embodied the cosmic system quite simply and was superior to every individual priest, by reason of the abundance of sanctity concentrated in his person. Livy tells how, shining far over the field of battle through the unique splendour of his royal raiment, Tolumnius, the *lucumo* of Veii, gallops ahead of his warriors.

To abolish a monarchy of this type was not simple. In Rome it continued to survive in the title of 'sacrifice king' (*rex sacrificulus*) and of *flamen dialis*. We cannot ascertain what was the corresponding development in Etruria. The enormous, richly furnished mound-tombs of the seventh century B.C., such as the Regolini-Galassi tomb, seem to bear witness to a sublime cult of kings. By their style the gold ornaments and the throne of Larthia can also be seen to belong to a world with the same beliefs, and to point to the dress and pageantry of the 'victor'. The evolution of the tomb-structures supports a theory that the families nearest to the *lucumones* were gaining in power, but the fact is that no comprehensive analysis of tomb furniture and design has yet been undertaken from the angle of social history.

Of the early constitution of the Confederation we really know nothing at all precise. It may be that there was one king at the head of the whole, of the style of Alcinous, the king of the Phaeacians, who says, in the 'Odyssey': 'For the leaders who rule over the people are twelve noble and illustrious princes, and I myself am the thirteenth among the others'. In the same way Tinia stands at the head of the eight thunderbolt-wielding gods as ninth and at the head of the twelve counselling divinities, the *Di consentes*, as thirteenth. Many reports allege that Porsenna was such a king over others.[1] The Roman lictors numbered twelve and this was attributed to the fact that in Etruria originally each of the twelve 'peoples' had appointed a judicial assistant to the king of the Confederation whom they had all elected together.

[1]Cf. p. 126.

Later it seems that a 'college', a *collegium*, governed the Confederation, but all these points are still unclear in detail.

Mezentius, King of Cerveteri

Only a very few names of kings have come down to us. Mezentius of Cerveteri, who is supposed to have been a contemporary of Aeneas, is painted, like Tarquinius Superbus, the last king of the Romans, in the dreadful colours normally used to depict tyrants. A recollection of his violent removal from the royal throne, but also of his incomparable heroism, lives in the lines of Virgil, in the 'Aeneid':—'After many years of prosperity came the rule of King Mezentius who suppressed the people with cruel weapons. Need I relate the horrible murders and savage deeds of the despot? May the gods keep him and his like for their own vengeance! Did he not even bind living bodies to corpses, hand to hand and face to face? Cruel torture! And thus let them die a lingering death, rotting into poison and slime in that horrible embrace. At length the citizens, weary of the cruel madman, seize weapons, surround his dwelling, slay the man himself and his servants and hurl fire on to his roof. He himself escapes from the slaughter into the land of the Rutulians. There he seeks shelter and the weapons of his friend and host, Turnus, give him protection. Thereupon all Etruria arises in bitter wrath, threatens war and demands the king for punishment.'

'But he stands like a rock which juts out into the sea and endures unshaken against the angry breakers and the threats of sea and sky. . . .'

'But Mezentius now shakes his mighty spear and marches furiously forward on the plain.'

The Last Kings

The monarchy seems to have been abolished in Tarquinii and Cerveteri some time between 510 and 490 B.C. But in Veii there were *lucumones* down to the second half of the fifth century B.C. This proves that the individual Etruscan cities could each determine and evolve their own constitution and social organization, without prejudice to their membership of the Confederation of the Twelve. Lars Tolumnius, king of Veii, is said to have been guilty, intentionally or not, through a misunderstood exclamation during a game of dice, of causing the Fidenates, deserters from Rome in 429 B.C., to commit the crime of murdering the ambassadors from Rome. One year later he fell in battle by the hand of the Roman consul Aulus Cornelius Cossus who had sworn, crying out loudly over the heads of the armies, to slay him as a sacrifice to the gods for those who had been murdered on his orders. With the decapitated head of the fallen man on the point of his lance Cossus forced his way through the rows of battle and thus drove the horrified Veientes and Fidenates off in panic flight. Livy says that the linen cuirass of the conquered king still hung in the time of the Emperor Augustus in the temple of Jupiter Feretrius in Rome, labelled with an old inscription.

Thereafter Veii also was governed by officials elected for a year: he who would be entrusted with the high office must woo the people.

Fig. 32. Tomb painting, first half of the fifth century B.C.

Nevertheless it seems not always to have been easy to come to an agreement, for it is said that scarcely a generation later the Veientes, disgusted by their difficulty in doing so, had, in the emergency of the war which had newly broken out with Rome, once again given themselves a king. Because of him, says Livy, the other Etruscans, meeting in the Confederation's shrine, refused to come to the help of the hard-pressed city, not only because they were against the whole institution of monarchy, but because in addition they hated the man elected by the Veientes.

His name is not known to us. Even before he became king, the Etruscans had been annoyed by the haughty arrogance of this wealthy

Veientian. He had competed for a post as priest at a meeting of the twelve peoples gathered in the grove of Voltumna, but had been defeated in the voting by another. His pride deeply hurt, he then committed the sacrilege of disturbing the inviolably sacred festival games, by withdrawing without previous notice all the actors, dancers, flautists and jugglers who belonged to him—no small number. This insult, says Livy, he inflicted on a people who, more than any other, were so devoted to everything which had to do with worship and religion that they had achieved a unique mastery of their practice and accordingly took note of even the slightest deviations or faults.

4. HOSTILE SYRACUSE

The Naval Battle off Cumae

In the year 474 B.C. the Etruscans suffered an annihilating defeat off Cumae at the hands of Hieron, the tyrant of Syracuse. Among the votive offerings which have been excavated in Olympia there is to be seen a simple bronze helmet, hemispherical in shape, an inscription on which indicates that it was part of the booty from this naval battle

Fig. 33. Etruscan helmet, votive gift offered by Hieron of Syracuse at Olympia 474 B.C.

131

(Fig. 33).[1] One wonders whether the Syracusan dedicated this Etruscan armour here in the great shrine of all the Hellenes (where he himself had twice won a victory in horse-racing and once with a four-in-hand chariot) on account of the fact that he attributed a pan-Greek significance to the destruction of the Tyrsenian fleet.

'Zeus, grant I beg thee that the battle cry of the Phoenicians and the Tyrsenians may be stilled! They have seen their agonized fleet repent of their insolence off Cumae and vanquished by the lord of the Syracusans, who flung their young warriors from their swift ships into the sea, thus protecting Hellas from grievous bondage. . . .'

So sings Pindar in the first of his 'Pythian Odes' to the renown of the Sicilian tyrant. In the same breath he names the victory won near Himera over the Carthaginians six years earlier by Gelon, the brother of the hero whose praises he is singing, and these two Syracusan successes he places on a par with the famous victories over the Persians won by mainland Hellenes in precisely those years near Plataea and Salamis.

And so we become witnesses of how a myth is created, for the battle for freedom of the Greeks against the Persians is seen as a world war occupying the whole Mediterranean region, and the Carthaginians and Etruscans regarded so to speak as the other flank of barbarism pressing on under Xerxes. Later historians took up this theme. There thus arose a picture of a powerful Etruscan federal state with the status of a large and centrally directed empire. Ultimately Livy could write that 'The power of Etruria was so great that the fame of its name filled the lands and seas from one end of Italy to the other, from the Alps to the straits of Messina'. But information of this sort is more interesting as evidence of the development of historical consciousness in ancient times, and of its continuing influence up to modern times, than as historical fact.

Etruscans and Carthaginians

The first evidence of an alliance of Etruscans and Carthaginians against Greeks is the Phocaean battle in Sardinian waters reported on by Herodotus. It was, as we have seen (p. 120), not aimed against the Greeks as such, but against the establishment of a foreign piratical power in a

[1]London, British Museum, discovered 1817. The dedicatory inscription is as follows: 'Ἰάρων ὁ Δεινομένεος καὶ τοὶ Συρακόσιοι τῷ Δὶ Τύραν' ἀπὸ Κύμας (Hieron, the son of Deinomenes, and the Syracusans: Tyrrhenian booty from Cumae to Zeus).

domain which Carthage and Cerveteri alike had come to regard as their own sphere of interest. A generation later, about 508 B.C., we find Rome, newly become a republic, concluding a similar treaty with the Carthaginians. We are quite well informed about its contents. The superiority of Carthage compared with the city on the Tiber, which at that time was in a state of weakness, is plain. The treaty, however, was primarily intended to define spheres of interests. Rome restricts her trade and refrains from voyaging in the western Mediterranean, while Carthage in return acknowledges the claim of the Romans to leadership in the coastal territory of Latium, without surrendering her own claim to do business there. It is obvious that the treaty is not so much aimed at any joint enterprises as at the acknowledgment of the Carthaginian claim to unimpeded naval supremacy and trade monopoly in the whole of the western Mediterranean area, and at the establishment of the Roman claim to supremacy in Latium. The Etruscans, reputedly Rome's chief enemies at that time, are not named.

This treaty shows the Carthaginians in possession of Sardinian harbours, in which they grant the Romans permission to trade though they reserve the right to practise certain controls. If the Carthaginians could already operate with such assurance in the old spheres of influence of the Tyrrhenians, then clearly the treaties made also with Tuscan cities were not based on the parity of two naval powers of equal fighting strength. It is true that according to Aristotle there were additional clauses which went beyond the agreements with the Romans and there were in existence understandings about imported goods, non-aggression treaties and written agreements to be brothers in arms. But treaties of this kind obviously also contained (and this is confirmed by objects excavated) the renunciation by the Etruscans of the Western maritime area claimed by the Carthaginians. The Etruscan coastal cities were not strong enough to drive the Phocaeans out of their immediate vicinity unaided. Their own forces were also not sufficient to enable them to maintain their link by sea with Hellas—a route which was first controlled by Aristodemus, the tyrant of Cumae, and then by Syracuse, and which was so important for their cultural and economic existence— and their connexion with Athens which was now coming more and more into the forefront. That is the reason why they joined with Carthage, in circumstances which are no longer clear in detail, and not because one naval power was seeking to make common cause with another in order to prevent the rise of a third, nor because a common hate of the Greeks had driven the two peoples, culturally so different, into partnership.

Syracuse Endangers the Links with Hellas

Etruria had never had a dispute with the Carthaginians so continuous and radical as with Hellas. But the imperialistic power politics of individual city-states in the Graeco-Italic colonial territories under the rule of tyrants imperilled Etruria's arteries leading to Hellas itself. The victory of the Syracusans off Cumae was not, as the Syracusan tyrant himself probably pictured it and by the consecration of his votive offering in Olympia proclaimed it, a victory over a barbarism which was endangering the freedom of Hellas, but rather confirmed the superiority of one single city-state which was striving for total power, and which claimed for itself the control of all seaborne traffic between western Italy and Greece, and which thereby made exceptionally difficult (though it did not completely stop) the direct contact between Attic Greece, just then entering its classic period, and Etruria.

What little we otherwise know of the relations between the Etruscans and Syracusans does not alter the picture. The Syracusan actions against Etruria ranked as skirmishes against pirates and in turn had as their object plunder and booty. The Etruscans at no time appeared with a challenge which could be interpreted, like the Carthaginian and Attic expeditions, as an attempt to overthrow Sicily or at least a part thereof. It is difficult to understand the position unless we remind ourselves that in the ancient world sea-trading and sea-raiding were scarcely distinguishable, and piracy was regarded as a natural and honourable way of earning a living. Nowhere is it recorded that these disputes were ever the subject of council meetings of the twelve cities at the shrine of Voltumna. There is not even evidence of a single joint operation by the coastal cities.

We learn that the Syracusans about the middle of the fifth century B.C. officially organized voyages to Elba and to the Tuscan coast in order to put a stop to the piratical practices of the Tyrrhenian sea robbers. Phayllos, the first admiral who was sent out, allowed himself to be bribed, but his successor, Apelles, conquered Elba, island of minerals, and successfully ravaged the Tyrrhenian shore.

An inscription in the Roman tongue recently found in Tarquinii, though unfortunately badly mutilated, tells of the brave operation of a Tarquinian admiral, who is described as a praetor, against Sicily. He is supposed on this venture to be the first who took his ships across the Tyrrhenian Sea, which probably means that he gave up the coastal route and ventured on the high seas. Unfortunately we cannot give this journey a more precise date than the period after the kings. It is an example of an enterprise carried out with public funds and commissioned by the state, by one single coastal city against the Sicilian obstructors of navigation routes. Whether the expedition was successful is not related.

Assistance to Athens

When in the year 414/13 B.C. the Athenians at the instigation of Alcibiades transferred the theatre of war to Sicily during the Peloponnesian war and looked around as far as Carthage for help against Syracuse, several Etruscan cities offered their support. Thucydides declares expressly that the Tyrsenians gave their promise 'on account of the existing dissension with Syracuse'. Only three fifty-oar ships actually turned up, but a little later their crews saved the situation by their glorious bravery in a critical moment of battle, and were therefore specially commemorated.

Finally the voyage undertaken against Etruria by the fleet of the Syracusan tyrant Dionysius in the year 384 B.C. is represented as primarily an operation of pillaging and revenge against Cerveteri. He needed money and so sailed north with sixty or according to other sources with one hundred triremes.[1] We do not know how far his plundering voyage took him nor all the places he visited, but his principal blow fell on Pyrgos, the port of Agylla (Cerveteri) whose name is Greek and which was probably largely inhabited by Greeks. The tyrant did not even pause before the shrine of the great goddess called Leucothea or Ilithyia in the reports, but took thence whatever he could find in gold and silver and valuable forged work. The treasure show-cases in the Etruscan museums give some idea of the works of art which were roughly lumped together here and carried off to the melting pots. The booty was said to be worth not less than a thousand talents

---

[1]Trireme = the most usual type of ship (including ship-of-war) of ancient times, a galley with three banks or rows of oars above one another on each side (German editor's note).

and the sale of the prisoners and other plundered goods piled into the ships brought in a further five hundred talents.

Etruria, though in contact in the Early Iron Age through the Phoenicians and the Greeks with the mighty traffic of the Mediterranean, was never able to thrust her way beyond her coastal waters, i.e. the sea bounded by the islands of Elba, Corsica and Sardinia which lay off her shores. At no time do we hear of the islands themselves being in her hands and there is no trace of any unified purposeful expansion beyond the seas by the forces of the Central Italian cities allied in the Confederation of the Twelve. To expect anything of the kind from the Etruscans is to measure them by the wrong standards and to deny them their individuality. The individual city, a holy autonomous formation founded on cosmic concepts, held its own within the limits of its strength. All that has been handed down to us about treaties and military operations proves that the Etruscans aimed at defending the individuality and the existence of the city-state and not at creating a great power. The characteristic of the Etruscans which we have already seen in their art we find here again: their tendency to cling to archaic ways of thought long after the Greeks and Carthaginians had developed an imperial policy, which was to start the Peloponnesian War in Greece and thus, by way of Syracuse, affect Etruria too.

CHAPTER VI

Rome or Veii

I. WAGING WAR THE OLD WAY

Disturbed Peace Between Neighbours

SIMILAR features are to be found in accounts of the fighting between Rome and Veii, the Etruscan royal city which lies three and a half hours' walk north of Rome on the right of what later became the Via Cassia. The conquest of Veii in the year 396 B.C. by the dictator Marcus Furius Camillus was a milestone in both Etruscan and Roman history. For it began a process which continued without interruption, and ultimately, in the first century B.C., led to the complete assimilation of Etruria in the territory of the Roman state.

The disputes between the two cities had already started in the time of the Roman kings. Simultaneously with regular and properly declared wars a criss-cross of plundering raids was always going on. In the intervals relations prevailed which Livy described as being neither war nor peace and rather like highway robbery. The same lawless conditions which had long reigned at sea now characterized the relations of these two neighbouring powers which never, during the whole period of their existence side by side, concluded any lasting formal treaty with one another. In Greece, according to the testimony of Thucydides, there were regions and tribes in which such conditions ruled as late as in the second half of the fifth century B.C. Piracy, cattle-stealing and plundering of open settlements—there is nothing dishonourable in this: on the contrary, these are all elements constituting in archaic noble society what might be called the free play of forces. Like the monarchy in Veii these ways of earning a living and these relationships have roots unusually deep in historical time.

Roving Army Leaders

The Etruscan army leaders whom we come across in the accounts
handed down were moulded by just such attitudes of mind and conditions of living. These heroes appear as adventurous knight-errants
who, for the sake of fame and booty, driven by friendship or a desire
for vengeance, set forth into distant lands with their brave and faithful
followers, in order to win power and then, diverted to new goals,
give it up again, as Porsenna is supposed to have done with Rome.
Legend has it that because of offended honour Aruns of Chiusi went
as far as Gaul in order to assemble an army against the powerful
people in his home town. It is supposed to be through him that
Brennus then came with his hordes to Central Italy and ultimately to
Rome.

From Vulci came the brothers Aulus and Caelius Vibenna, of whom
it is related that they led their warriors against Rome. When one of
them had fallen, his friend Mastarna, who was later identified with
Servius Tullius, was said to have carried the operation to a successful
conclusion and in memory of his lost comrade to have named one of
the seven hills of the Eternal City Caelius. This whole story probably
originates in Etruscan tradition for one of the murals of the *Tomba
François* in Vulci, painted about the turn of the fourth and third
centuries B.C., shows 'Macstrna' among groups of fighting heroes
whose names are all written in the margin. He is liberating, in a bold
and sudden attack, his friend 'Caile Vipinas' who is held in bonds by
the enemies, also the friend's brother 'Avle' and still another warrior,
depicted also among those taken by surprise who are being cruelly
mown down, namely a certain 'Cneve Tarchumies Rumach'—Gnaeus
Tarquinius of Rome—which seems to transfer the events in the Vul-
cientian version also to the period of the Tarquinian dynasty. But it was
only the discovery of a Bucchero fragment ascribable to the second
half of the sixth century B.C. in the so-called sanctuary of Apollo
at Veii which recently turned this legendary event into a reality
and simultaneously connected it with the Etruscan rival of Rome.
The engraved words declare that 'Avile Vipiiennas', whom we can
hardly dissociate from the Aulus Vibenna whose existence is vouched
for in literature, deposited a votive offering here in the Veientian
sanctuary.

National Wars and Private Wars

With this background, things which are otherwise not easily understood in the reports of the Veientian fighting become comprehensible.
The Etruscan Confederation stubbornly refuses to enter into the war in
its own name or to involve all its members, but it authorizes the young
people to go to the help of the Veientes as volunteers at their own discretion. For long years Rome fears a joint attack by all the Etruscans
and in the Confederation's assemblies feeling among the Tyrrhenians
is shown as distinctly hostile to Rome, yet when famine holds sway the
Romans send as a matter of course to Etruria for deliveries of grain and
in every case receive them. Traders and artisans also ply undisturbed
between Rome and the shrine of Voltumna even throughout the
period of the disputes.

We learn from an incident which may be described as the Fabian
episode that Rome herself was able to distinguish between official and
private warfare, even in the fifth century B.C. This was an occasion
when one single powerful family undertook a separate war against
Veii out of revenge for the death of one of its members, Quintus Fabius.
Three hundred and six members of the Fabian clan set forth, with their
own arms and their own steeds, to lay waste and plunder the lands of
the enemy. They made their quarters in a camp on the banks of the
lower Cremera which a little higher up flows round the territory of the
city of Veii. Decoyed by cunningly driven herds of cattle they fell into
an ambush and everyone of them was slain by the hail of arrows of the
Etruscans, except the youngest who was spared to act as messenger to
bear home the news of the defeat.

In Greece it was not until the close of the sixth century B.C. that a
distinction was drawn between private and national campaigns and the
state accepted any responsibility for freebooting carried on by its
citizens. In that country this marks the end of the archaic period, and
the birth of a new political thinking, closely bound up with events in
the classical era of Hellenism. In Etruria and also in Rome the old ways
of thinking had a very much longer life. Even as late as the end of the
fourth century B.C. it was possible for one thousand Etruscans to be in
the Punic army in Sicily while on the other hand when Agathocles,
ruler of Syracuse, who was otherwise hostile to Etruscans, was pressed
by the same Carthaginians, eighteen ships were dispatched from

Etruria to his aid. Of course the world of classical Greece was not unknown to the Etruscans. All the same its influence was felt not so much as a force affecting life as a whole but rather, both in art and in other spheres, as an inspiration in individual instances.

2. REASONS FOR HOSTILITY

Whatever grounds have been advanced for the quarrels and fights between Veii and Rome during the course of a century and a half, the real cause lies not in the differences of language or race of the two rival powers, nor even in an irreconcilable religious antagonism. After all, the relationship of the city on the Tiber to its other Tyrrhenian neighbour, Cerveteri, was always good, apart from a few small incidents. Indeed the Romans actually sent their sons there that they might learn from the masters of the priesthood the perfect manner of praying and sacrificing, and above all of soothsaying, and when the Gauls invaded Rome in 387/386 B.C. the Romans evacuated some of their idols and priests and Vestal Virgins to Cerveteri where they found a hospitable reception and practised their own form of worship for a considerable time without restrictions. Why was a similar relationship with Veii not possible?

It is true that Rome lay like a barrier between Veii and the sea. The great part played in the fighting by Fidenae, situated on the Roman side of the Tiber opposite the Etruscan city, suggests that it was a question of possession of the river and of the roads running inland through the valley, and of access to the sea and the saltponds. Veii's heyday in the seventh and sixth centuries B.C. is unthinkable without strong connexions with Greece, judging by the vases, the wall-paintings and the great terracottas in the *Grotta Campana*. The products of the interior, particularly grain and timber, but also precious ore, were transported by ship down the Tiber to almost before the city gates. The growth and expansion of Roman power endangered the very foundations of Veii's legendary wealth.

On the other hand, as the population of Rome increased, the destruction of Veii inevitably became a matter of life and death for her. It was probably the failure of Veii to recognize this when at the height of her own power, and to forestall the rise of such a close and populous rival, which caused her downfall, despite all the heroism later displayed. However, during the period when such decisions should have been made, Etruscan ways of thinking and of living, as we have seen, continued to follow old-fashioned lines.

It is possible that in Latium aridity and soil deterioration had already set in in the fifth century B.C., caused by pillage of the forests and a ruthless form of land utilization, and that the irrigation and drainage system had already fallen into disorder. However, it can be regarded as certain that Rome's development into a large city posed the Romans a number of problems which they had to face without previous experience. The numerous epidemics and famines of which we read in the annals of Rome prove this. The feeding of an evergrowing population, which in spite of treaties with the Carthaginians was able to take only a very limited part in the struggle of Graeco-Punic forces which governed overseas trade, and was moreover on account of its internal structure not designed for it, demanded peremptorily the acquisition of fertile lands, the expulsion or annihilation of existing proprietors and the securing of the Tiber as the route from the interior by which grain was supplied. The events which followed the conquest of Veii proved this with the utmost clarity.

The free-born were sold, the lands were divided up. A fierce dispute arose among the citizens of Rome, for one strong party demanded emphatically that the dwellings on the Tiber be given up and that they move into the much more beautiful Veii, situated amidst rich agricultural land. Others proposed that a double city be founded and the patricians should live in the city of the seven hills, the plebeians in Veii. After the destruction of Rome by the Gauls the debate received fresh impetus. Many Romans migrated of their own volition to the abandoned city. The outward movement was halted only when the mighty Marcus Furius Camillus, victor over Veientes and Gauls, appealed solemnly to religious powers and obligations and when a chance word of a Roman centurion was interpreted as a sign from the gods, while in addition the severest punishment was threatened for anyone who settled in the Etruscan stronghold which the gods themselves had given up. Veii had to fall because Rome needed her lands in order to feed her own population and needed free navigation on the Tiber, this 'river, so fortunately bedded that it brings down the fruits of the earth to us from the interior and receives our imports at the sea' as Camillus is reported by Livy to have said.[1]

[1] As early as 474 B.C. the Veientes had had to deliver grain as well as money in order to obtain a forty-year truce.

3. PROPHECY AND DESTINY
The Waters of the Alban Lake

Knowing the importance attributed by the Etruscans to foretelling the future by means of liver scrutiny and soothsaying, and knowing all we do about their belief in destiny, we cannot be surprised that they saw the fall of Veii also as the fulfilment of a doom foreseen and foretold by the experts. The Tagetic doctrine taught that there was no way of escaping such events ordained by the forces of destiny, though there was always the possibility of achieving a postponement. Such a belief must have had a paralysing effect on the fighting powers of a population attacked by ruthless opponents in a life or death struggle. It is understandable that the king did all he could to hush up speeches and pronouncements which affected the fate of the city.

In the penultimate year before the siege the gods sent a number of alarming portents. At first little attention was paid to these in Rome because only individuals reported about them and above all because, as Livy confirms, during the current dissensions with the Etruscans, there were no *haruspices* available who knew how to study such signs and to interpret them. Then, however, great and universal apprehension was aroused by the news that the waters of the Alban Lake at the foot of Mons Albanus, the sacred mountain of Latium, which is still to this day unpredictable in its movements, had begun to rise, without unusually heavy rain having fallen or there being any other reason, and had already reached an abnormal level. Messengers were sent to Delphi, to ask the Pythoness for her advice. However, before they returned an Etruscan seer fell into the hands of the Romans. Even though this story is related by Livy in the style of a romance, it does in its broad outlines coincide too well with other accounts and fit too well the *haruspices* and their way of interpreting signs for us to reject it as an invention.

'As the sentinels of the Roman army were once again passing the time under the walls of Veii with jokes and teasing each other, they heard a Tyrrhenian singing in prophetic tones to announce that never would the Romans overcome the city before the waters of Lake Alban had been drained.' At first his words were not taken really seriously, then the listeners began to talk them over till at last one of the sentinels in the course of a gossip with Veientes on the other side of the border (as had been customary on account of the long duration of the siege) learned that the strange speaker was a *haruspex*. The Roman, himself not indifferent to the world of the sacred, sought a conversation with the grey seer. He let him be told that he needed his advice as he had received a sign from the gods which he could not understand. The two met unarmed away from the troops. Suddenly the stalwart young man seized the feeble old one and dragged him into the Roman camp in front of all eyes and despite the powerless protests of the Veientes. He

Fig. 34. Demon of death, tomb painting, early fourth century B.C.

was brought before the generals then before the Senate. The fathers asked him for the meaning of his strange saying.

'The gods must have been angry with the Veientes on that day,' said the prisoner, 'when they drove him to reveal the fall of the city of his fathers which was destined by fate. He could not now take back what he then said in a holy transport. Indeed he would perhaps be committing no less a crime if he now withheld that which the immortals wanted to be known, than if he announced what properly he ought to keep silent. In the books of destiny (*Libri fatales*) and the doctrine of the Etruscans (*Disciplina Etrusca*) it was recorded that if once the Alban waters were to rise and be drained off by the Romans in the ritually correct manner, then Veii was condemned to fall. Before then however the gods would not surrender the walls of the Veientes. Thereupon he explained the manner in which the lake must be diverted in accordance with the will of the gods.'

The Roman city fathers did not like to rely on the utterances of one single man but decided to await the return of the messengers sent to Delphi. When these returned, the reply of the Greek oracle coincided with the prophecies of the Etruscan. The lake must no longer confine the Alban water, declared the Pythoness; yet it must also not be allowed to flow freely to the sea; the Romans must so divert its floods that they moistened far and wide the fields over which it must be artificially distributed till it had disappeared—then Rome would obtain a victory over Veii. The reputation of the Veientian *haruspex* rose mightily after this corroboration by Delphi. His instructions on how to divert the lake and on propitiation and the revival of neglected religious ceremonies and ritual rules, were followed.

We may regard this linking of the fate of Veii, on the right bank of the Tiber, with the Alban Lake, twenty-eight miles away and moreover on the other side of the river, as being quite arbitrary, or we may see in it a useful pointer for Rome to the necessity, as a condition for victory, that she should first secure through planned irrigation the rehabilitation of her own Latin lands and thus establish sound agricultural foundations. In any case the whole style of the story even to the dilemma of the *haruspex* between the duty to make known and the wish to conceal is a clear example of Etruscan attitudes as manifested both here and in other fragmentary examples.[1]

In this way the prophecy and its fulfilment are so closely interwoven that they become mutually essential. Similarly we are told that those who have the terrible gift of second sight have a horror of their own vision, for they are unable to judge how far events actually happen because of their utterances which they would be glad to suppress but yet dare not leave unsaid.

The Last Sacrifice in Veii

The story of the last sacrifice offered in Veii and its connexion with

[1]For the connexion between a pronouncement made as a result of an inner compulsion and the actual events, i.e. the problem of the 'magical coupling' and the irrevocability of the utterance cf. the Vulcatius episode on pp. 1 and 20.

Plate XV.   The head of a Warrior. Veii. About 500 B.C.

(By courtesy of Kohlhammer Verlag, Stuttgart)

Plate XVI.   A Terracotta statue of the Goddess Diana. Fifth century B.C.

(By courtesy of Kohlhammer Verlag, Stuttgart)

the fall of the city sounds less credible. Admittedly Livy himself draws attention to its extreme antiquity, but he relates it only with reserve. Whether it is true or not, it conforms to such an extent to the Etruscan attitude towards fulfilment of destiny that it is still worthy of mention. According to Etruscan ideas, of course, the reason for the conquest of such a city could not possibly lie in the superiority of Roman arms or in the confusion caused by the enemy breaking out from a secretly constructed subterranean corridor. For them the cause was rather the will of the gods which makes itself known in advance by recognizable portents and which, discovered by experts from the liver of a sacrificial animal, from the flight of the birds or some other special event and made known by them, is irresistibly fulfilled.

'This' said Seneca in a frequently quoted passage of his *Quaestiones Naturales* 'is what distinguishes us (the Romans) from the Tuscans, masters in the observation of lightning. We think that lightning arises because clouds bump against each other; they on the other hand hold the belief that the clouds bump together only in order that lightning may be caused. For as they connect everything with God they have the notion that lightning is not significant on account of its appearance as such, but that it only appears at all because it has to give divine signs.'

The Roman general had had men working day and night to construct a tunnel which led underground right into the principal shrine of the Veientes, the temple of Uni (Juno), situated on the citadel. It appears credible that the Roman warriors emerging like demons of the underworld out of the earth spread terror and made it possible for the Roman armies to force open the gates of the city in a swift attack and to press in from outside in a flood. Women and slaves flung down pieces of stone and tile from the roofs of the burning houses. The cries and wails of children and women mingled with the noise of battle. All who resisted the intruders were mown down and massacred.

The catastrophe is supposed to have begun when the king of Veii was making a sacrifice and the *haruspex* prophesied that he who laid the entrails of this sacrificial animal before the gods would win the victory. Penned in the dark earthen corridor of the tunnel and waiting for the command of their general, the Roman soldiers heard this. They broke out, stole the entrails and brought them to Marcus Furius Camillus. This was the deed which decided the fall of Veii.

Fig. 35. Entrance to a tomb near Veii, the *Grotta Campana*, second half of the seventh century B.C.

4. DEPARTURE OF THE CITY DIVINITY

But now it becomes plain that in this battle it had not been merely a question of defeating an unpleasant and envied rival. Veii, like any Etruscan city established according to ritual, was both more than and other than a fortified residential community of proprietors, and this was known to the attacking Romans, or at any rate to the Roman general who is described as particularly experienced in religious matters. He vowed before the last attack to offer one-tenth of all booty to the Delphic Apollo; he promised to institute large-scale games to be repeated annually; but above all, and this is what appears to be the most important point, he bound himself with a sacred oath to erect for the patron goddess of the city of Veii, the Queen Uni (Juno Regina), a new temple worthy of her in Rome, if she were willing to abandon the Veientes and be transferred to Rome.

When the fighting was over it was very plain what all this meant. The booty was carried away from the private houses and the public buildings. Then they started to empty the temples too, and to take away the votive gifts, indeed the gods themselves. The Apollo of Veii, the Hermes, the goddess with the child and the other wonderful large terracottas in the *Villa Giulia* in Rome, which appear to us as masterpieces of the archaic sculpture of the Etruscans, were now carelessly thrown down from the temple roof and fell among the rubbish. They were not objects of worship but mere earthenware roof ornaments and votive gifts and to them was attributed neither special intrinsic value nor protective sanctity. But in order to escort the sacred effigy of the Queen Uni to Rome they chose the most perfect youths out of the whole Roman army.

The young Romans were made to bathe and to put on white robes before they reverently entered the shrine. Somewhat timidly they laid their hands on the statue which till then, according to Etruscan practice, could not be touched by anyone at all other than its own priest who belonged to a certain family. Whether impelled by a divine command or by mere youthful levity, one of the youths asked 'Wilt thou go to Rome, Juno?' 'She has nodded yes!' cried all the others, and later it was even said that she had replied with an audible voice that she would go. In any case she allowed herself to be lifted without trouble from the place where she had hitherto stood and to be brought voluntarily and without incident to Rome. Four years later the Temple of Juno Regina was consecrated to her on the Aventine, as Camillus had vowed, and it is said that women in particular did all they could to glorify the festival of this temple consecration.

It may be remembered that other Etruscan cities also were dedicated through their names to a divinity. As the Veientes belonged to the Queen Uni, so the men of Populonia (Pupluna) belonged to Fufluns (Dionysus), those of Mantua, the capital of the North Etruscan Confederation to Mantus god of death, and similarly probably the Volsinians to Veltune (Voltumna), the Tarquinians to the hero Tarchon whose

Fig. 36. Tomb painting, late sixth century B.C.

name may likewise conceal some old Etruscan divinity. Whether the Etruscan Confederation as a whole can be seen as a reflected counterpart of a community of gods in which each city is as it were the house of one of the twelve gods, we do not know. But the remarkable account of the removal of the divine Queen Uni to Rome makes it probable that the conquest and extinction of Veii involved serious damage to the structure of the Etruscan Confederation as a whole.

It is possible that the loss was made good by the ceremonial acceptance of one of the other cities which satisfied all the religious conditions. But the fact that it could happen at all and that it was possible for the remaining cities, despite all Veii's efforts to drag the Confederation as a whole into the war, to intervene so little in these events while there was still time to do so and Rome might still have been contained, demonstrates that the other Etruscans did not foresee how the Romans would act and did not recognize in time Rome's significance for their own existence. This underlines once again what other reports also make known, namely that the Confederation was not a body consisting of powers with a policy aimed at certain goals and developing dynamically, but a union of an old-fashioned kind based on religion and worship and deeply rooted in magical conceptions.

CHAPTER VII

The End of Etruria

I. THE GAULS INVADE THE PLAIN OF THE PO

The Northern Etruscan Confederation

Among the reasons advanced, according to Livy, by the representatives of the Etruscan Confederation in the shrine of Voltumna at Volsinii, against a united intervention of the twelve cities against Rome during the Veientian War, was a reference to the danger which threatened Etruria anew from the Gauls. These are at that date referred to as a people who as yet had never been seen and with whom neither a secure peace nor a declared war existed. On the very day on which Veii was taken by the Romans the Gallic tribes of Insubres, Boii and Semnones are alleged to have conquered and destroyed Melpum, the wealthy Etruscan city situated in the plain of the Po.

From reports and recollections of this kind it is clear that an impression was formed even in ancient times that the Confederation of Etruscan cities had fallen before the fatefully co-ordinated pressure of the Gauls from the north and the Romans from the south. 'Thus it was willed by the benevolent gods of Rome' says Karl Otfried Müller in his work on the Etruscans which appeared in 1828–31. 'Tuscan power which had ruled over Rome and Latium in the second century (of Roman history) had to be divided, occupied and weakened, yet at the same time still kept just strong enough to fend off conquering Gallic troops, except for isolated raiding parties, from Rome; meanwhile Rome sometimes united the Latin, Sabine and Oscan tribes around her, sometimes oppressed them, until she was strong enough to compel Etruria herself to recognize her "*majestas*" and then, in association with Etruria, to make an end completely to Italy's dread of the Gauls.'

But this interpretation of these events has only limited validity. No Central Italian city was so seriously affected by the Gauls as Rome herself. When the Gauls invaded Tuscany the Etruscans do not appear

Fig. 37. Tomb painting, about 520 B.C.

to have gone out to meet them, any more than they did the Romans, as a nation, a compact alliance combining all the forces of the territory under a unified command.

On the other hand the Confederation of northern Etruscan cities received irreparable damage from the invasion of the Gauls: for all practical purposes it succumbed and was never able to rise again. So far as we know the Etruscans who were centred on the Voltumna cult afforded no more aid to those in the plains of the Po than they did to Veii when she pleaded for help. There are also no grounds for the assumption that the Tuscan cities of northern Italy had populations more homogeneous than those in Tuscany proper. Virgil, as already mentioned, expressly refers to the mixed population of Mantua, the leader of the Confederation (cf. p. 33). When the Adriatic town of Spina, recently rediscovered in the delta marsh-land around Comacchio, has been excavated, we may be able to say more about the peculiar characteristics of such a northern Etruscan city. The mere fact of its situation in the flat land must have differentiated it from the cities of central Etruria which lay on the cliffbound tuff plateau. Near Marzabotto too, on the Bologna–Florence route, remains of wall foundations and of streets of a city have been discovered which seems to have been laid out in the fifth century B.C. in accordance with the rules of the Etruscan doctrine regarding the founding of a city.

We still know only very little of this Confederation of northern Etruscan cities. It is clear that it was a world complete in itself and independent, with its own history, and that it could not by any means be called a northern province of Central Etruria. What the two confederations had in common emerges above all in myths about the founding of cities, each of the individual cities being regarded as having been founded by Etruscan heroes of the type of a Porsenna or a Caile Vipina. The natural surplus of the population of Etruria overflowed to the north and to the south. Once again the Etruscans' adherence to very ancient notions and customs comes to the fore, for this emigration did not take the form of colonization. Instead, it was a movement in the style of some rite of spring or of the adventurous enterprises of some knight-commander who attracted bands to himself and undertook excursions into distant lands—customs which the Greeks also originally followed and, it is said, the ancient Italic peoples too. It appears that one of the essential reasons for Rome's superiority over the other Italic peoples and also over the Etruscans was the fact that she developed at a relatively early date other methods of controlling her population surplus.

We shall hardly go wrong if we regard the Confederation of cities grouped round Virgil's home town Mantua in the north and similarly the one round Capua in the south rather as the outcome of a type of culture and civilization which had grown up in Tuscany in the particular conditions of the seventh century B.C. than as the result of a national expansion. The unifying element in each seems to have been not so much common blood and uniform origin as their religion and the written language and script associated with that religion. The celebrated bronze liver found in Piacenza, a model which served for the training of priests and the teaching of the art of soothsaying with aid of sacrificial livers, bears witness to the significance of the Tagetic doctrine, the *Disciplina Etrusca*, for the north as well as in Etruria proper. Similarly there was a tradition that the twelve cities were founded by the same Tarchon under whose ploughshare Tages, the son of the Genius, emerged from the earth and chanted his wisdom to the holy ploughman and the priests whom he had summoned thither.

The Gauls in the Plain of the Po

Into this north Etruscan world Gallic tribal groups and hordes from southern France and the northern foothills of the Alps thrust from the close of the fifth century B.C. onwards. The era had dawned of the great Celtic migratory movements reaching as far as Greece and Asia Minor and in isolated cases as far as southern Italy. There is no record of the Confederation of northern Etruscan cities ever having offered resistance as a united whole. Individual Etruscan settlements seem indeed to have survived in Mantua and probably elsewhere, and a process of assimilation and interchange was initiated, but on the whole it is true that the greater part of the Po plain became Gallic within a few decades—Gallia Cisalpina, Gaul on this side of the Alps, as the Romans called it. Here and there a Tuscan heritage was preserved including for example the alphabet, from which later the Germani who advanced into the same area derived their runic script. We have, however, little detailed information about all these events.

The seizure of land by the Gauls in the Po plain gave rise to a state of constant danger for the cities of Etruria proper and above all for those situated on the great inland road to the south—Bologna–Fiesole–Arezzo –Cortona–Chiusi–Orvieto–Rome. The possibility of reconciliation and integration may not have been so unlikely here. There is after all good reason to assume an internal intimacy between the Hallstatt cultures of the northern Alps out of which Celtic civilization emerged and the Villanova culture which in the Early Iron Age formed the basis of Etruscan civilization. The real danger was that a border region, hitherto relatively peaceful, and dotted with cultural centres which were related to one another and to a certain extent conscious of this relationship, a region which had hitherto rather been threatened by Central Italy than threatening to it, had suddenly been transformed into an overflowing cauldron full of hordes of men stirred into movement. Uprooting themselves from their overpopulated homeland, these Gauls pushed each other forward and pressed on, ready each day to give up the place they had reached the previous day, into the fertile rich land from which glittering ornaments and equipment and splendid weapons had been coming to them for generations.

In his account of the seizure of land by the Gauls in the plain of the Po, Livy refers expressly to the attraction which the delicious fruits of the land and above all the wine exercised on these Nordic peoples. We hear of the troops of Brennus demanding gold and golden utensils from the conquered Romans, and the Gauls being prepared for the sake of Etruscan gold to fight side by side with the Arretinians against Rome or at least to leave the Etruscans in peace. In Chiusi, however, they demanded land on which to settle, claiming that the Clusini possessed more land than they actually needed.

2. BRENNUS BELEAGUERS CHIUSI AND ROME
Gallic Hordes in Central Italy

All this happened in the year 387/386 B.C. Brennus, prince of the Gallic Semnones, lay with a mighty army before Chiusi, and although

Rome had only just before defeated and destroyed Veii, slain its inhabitants or sold them into bondage, and carried off the sacred image of Juno Regina to the Aventine, it was to Rome that the Clusini turned for aid and not to the Confederation or to one of the other Etruscan cities. Nothing could show more plainly how wrong it is to talk of a national enmity between Etruscans and Romans. It is true that for some time after the fall of Veii there was emphatic talk at the assemblies in the grove of Voltumna of joint operations against Rome: nevertheless, Chiusi, one of the most honoured cities of the Confederation, which the name of Porsenna made famous, entered into negotiations with the allegedly hereditary enemy. The latter actually sent envoys who were probably intended at first only to inform themselves about the situation; but then, after an attempt had been made at conciliation between the disputants which miscarried on account of their obstinacy as regards both their own demands and their rejections of the other's offers, the emissaries personally intervened in the dispute in favour of the Etruscans.

Whether this was the real reason why Brennus gave up the siege of Chiusi and, infuriated by the breach of the sacred law which forbade envoys to take sides and participate in disputes, made off towards Rome disregarding all the Etruscan cities which lay on the way, we do not know. Clearly the surprise attack on the city by the Tiber, still glowing with pride from its recent victories, succeeded and the Gauls, after a victory over the hastily massed troops of the Romans, won an entrance into the city more because the inhabitants panicked than through storming the walls or through force, and then immediately made their way through the streets and houses burning and plundering. Many Romans fled to take shelter behind the walls of deserted Veii; others, carrying some of their shrines, took refuge in the neighbouring Etruscan city, Cerveteri. Those who stayed behind withdrew on to the Capitol and defended themselves from there.

The siege lasted seven months, for the Gauls were not capable of capturing the citadel rocks. Plague struck at the attackers from the ruined houses and irrigation installations. The air was filled with the horrible smell of corpses entrusted to the fire. Finally Brennus withdrew to the north, unharmed and laden with rich booty, partly because he had begun to despair of ever carrying the siege to a successful conclusion and partly because he was summoned home to the other side of the Alps by his fellow countrymen who had remained behind and were being threatened by the Veneti.

Not till a quarter of a century later, in 361 B.C., did the Gallic hordes again press as far south as Latium. Then indeed some of them got as far as Campania, though they were unable to achieve any permanent success there. They were defeated by the Romans although they allied themselves with Tibur and somewhat later with Praeneste which was at that time rebelling against Roman rule. It cannot be said that the differences between Romans and Latins and Samnites were less than or of a dissimilar kind from those between them and Etruscans. Each from time to time entered into agreements with the Gauls and at this very moment we find Rome concluding her second treaty with Carthage.

The Security of the Cities on the Rocks

The scanty success of the Gauls in Central Italy becomes understandable when one looks more closely at the situation of the settlements they were coming up against and their methods of attack. The cities of southern Etruria lie on long extended inaccessible rocky plateaux surrounded by canyon-like ravines cut deeply into the tuff i.e. *'fossi'*. The cities of the north, prominent on their mountain tops, are no less protected: Arezzo, Cortona, Perugia, Volterra, Populonia, Vetulonia and Rusellae; all were enclosed by strongly constructed walls, whose remains are to this day impressive evidence of their former strength.

The Gallic hordes were not in a position to capture such cities. Their armament, their fighting technique and customs were based on man-to-man encounters in skirmishes and in open battle. Even Rome succeeded ultimately in penetrating into the interior of the fortress of Veii more through cunning and luck than through storming by assault. In order to do this she had to defray the cost of besieging the town for several years, to improvise winter shelters for the soldiers during the hard time of the year when it had not hitherto been the custom to conduct war, to learn the science of mining, and to introduce a system of pay for the army. The Gauls might in a wild attack overwhelm the armies which flung themselves against them, but the cities remained safe from them except when chance or stupidity on the part of the citizens laid the way open, as in Rome. The Capitoline hill remained impregnable to Brennus and his troops.

The Tuscan cities were so spacious that they enclosed within their boundaries a part of the cultivable land belonging to the citizens. When in addition they had been adequately furnished with supplies by their community these cities could await with a certain degree of calm the end of a siege undertaken with insufficient means by an enemy not prepared for long delays and not able to storm walls, and the ultimate withdrawal of the plunderers out of the surrounding lands.

Attempts to Buy off the Enemy and to Form Alliances

The Gauls' incursions nevertheless caused enough damage— crippling of traffic and commercial relations, destruction or diminution of harvests and such other kinds of trouble and misfortune as foreign invaders usually bring to any country. So it is easy to understand that people sought to buy themselves free. Livy relates how in the year 301 B.C. the Etruscans tried by means of money to divert the Gauls from themselves and to drive them to annoy the Romans. The Gauls parleyed, accepted the payment offered, then at the last minute declared that they had entered into no further obligation than to leave Etruria in peace. If, however, the Tuscans would assure them cultivable land and settled homes in their territory, then they would be prepared to march against Rome. They were not interested in obtaining any other concession.

As the Etruscans did not consent, the Gauls withdrew, taking with them all the goods they had already received and leaving their trading partner behind, swindled. On the other hand Polybius' account of joint operations of Gauls and Tyrrhenians against Rome teaches us how illogical and lacking in unanimity the Tuscan attitude was in general. He tells too how on another occasion, in the year 283 B.C., the Arretinians sought Rome's protection against the Gallic besiegers, as the Clusini had earlier done.

As Rome waxed in strength in every direction, so the Etruscan cities in the north declined. This is not the place to expound the process in detail. Essentially it scarcely differed from that other parallel process which gradually brought under Rome's dominion her neighbours living south of the Tiber, the Latins and the Samnites. Moreover occasionally the Romans had to deal with alliances of several Etruscan cities, also with joint action by Etruscans and Gauls or even Samnites. It appears that a Confederation army embracing the entire Tuscan people was assembled on only two occasions and then only in a special way which is described below (cf. pp. 159 et seq.). So far as is known to-day there never was at any time either a peace treaty which might have been binding on all Etruria or one in which the Confederation of the Twelve Cities figured as a treaty partner. The different agreements showed great variety in the type and degree of relationships which they covered, varying from incorporation to provisional non-intervention agreements.

3. ROME REACHES OUT TOWARDS THE NORTH
Battles for Sutri and Nepi

For a long time the struggles between Romans and Etruscans which set in after the fall of Veii had as their main object possession of the east-west link, which follows the contours of the countryside between the middle reaches of the Tiber and the Tyrrhenian Sea. To-day this is represented by the stretch of light railway which leads from Orte in the southern foothills of the wooded Ciminian mountain range (Monte Cimini) through Capranica and on to Civitavecchia past the mountain hamlets of Barbarano Romano with San Giuliano and Bieda, famous for their monumental rock-cemeteries.

Cerveteri, situated south of the line, close to the sea, maintained friendly relations with Rome, except for one incident during which a part of her citizenry joined the Tarquinians who were attacking Roman territory along the coast. Rome and Tarquinii had thus no common frontiers in that area. Far more bitter was the struggle for possession of Sutrium (Sutri) and Nepete (Nepi), two places situated north of the former Veii, which are described by Livy as being positively the 'barriers and gateways' into Etruria (or contrariwise from there into Roman territory). Whoever possessed them had the way free to Tarquinii in the west, to Falerii (Città Castellana) in the east (which can blockade all traffic up the Tiber), southwards towards Rome, and northwards, if he penetrated the forest-clad mountains in the direction of the Vetralla of to-day, into the territory of Viterbo and Lake Bolsena, the heart of Etruria. This situation explains the close co-operation of Falerii and Tarquinii. For the Romans of those days Tarquinii became a name to fear.

The details of the armistice agreements concluded and then broken again, the plundering raids and laying waste, the revolts, victories and defeats in these struggles no longer seem very important. But the dispute between Rome and Etruria entered into a new and decisive phase when the consul Quintus Fabius, after winning a victory near Sutrium against the will or at least without the consent of the Senate, led his army diagonally through the Ciminian forest to the north, disdaining the passable roads. That was in the year 310 B.C.

The Conquest of the Forest-Clad Ciminian Mountains

Livy's account of this adventurous expedition into the high mountain forests conveys such a feeling of dread that it makes us think of the fairy tales of the brothers Grimm. The theme of the crossing of the boundary between Mitgard and Utgard, between the homeland and the outer world, is plainly recognizable. The fact that the Romans transformed it into a myth is an indication of how deeply this event itself stirred them.

'Even more pathless and frightening than were the mountains of Germania' says Livy, was the Ciminian forest at that time, and not even a trader had hitherto entered it. Then the brother of the consul, named Marcus Fabius, who in other versions is called Caeso or is described under the name Caius Claudius as stepbrother on his mother's side, set off to obtain information. He had, as was then customary, received a part of his education while lodging with hosts in Cerveteri and there learned not only the religious doctrines of the Etruscans but also their language. Along with a slave, who had grown up with him and been educated with him, he wandered disguised as a shepherd into the enemy country. Each carried a sickle and two Gallic spears and when they met country people they asked only the minimum of questions. But they were protected more by the fact that the Etruscans were unsuspecting than by any prudence and disguise, for the latter could not imagine for a moment that any foreigner would venture so deep into the wooded mountains.

In this manner these scouts are said to have penetrated as far as the Camertinian Umbrians, i.e. to Chiusi, without let or hindrance. There they made themselves known. How deep an impression their arrival made can be guessed by the fact that the Chiusi senate, i.e. the highest council of one of the most respected of the Twelve Cities, in the midst of a war which reputedly bound all the peoples of Etruria in a sacred conspiracy, declared itself ready to support the Roman army for a period of one month with food and men if it succeeded in penetrating as far as Chiusi. One is reminded of the alliance of the Clusini with Rome at the time of the first Gallic invasion.

With this assurance and well-informed about routes and terrain, the consul Quintus Fabius, skilfully evading the Etruscan outposts, slipped with his army at night to the heights of the Ciminian forest. Early in the morning after surveying the fertile fields of Etruria from there he sent his soldiers down into the country. They collected much plunder, drove to flight a few parties of ill-armed peasants hastily assembled by the nobility of the region, but, says Livy 'the war had rather been stirred up than fought out'. Even the hitherto peaceable Umbrians in the vicinity rose up against Rome and rendered assistance to the Etruscans.

A bold, carefully prepared surprise manoeuvre at first dawn (just the moment when in summer nights all are accustomed to lie in deepest sleep) gave the Roman commander a victory of such convincing decisiveness that Perugia, Cortona, and Arretium begged in Rome for peace and an alliance. Approximately 60,000 of the enemy are said to have fallen or been taken prisoner. The heart of Etruria was to become the scene of further events.

Livy's account of these occurrences contains various inaccuracies and contradictions, so that it remains uncertain how far the two other victories of Quintus Fabius in Etruria, announced as taking place in the same year, are really separate operations. A battle of fearful bitterness is said to have been fought on Lake Vadimon. The position of this little sulphur lake, which occupies an old volcanic crater an hour's walk further north from Orte and not far from the right bank of the Tiber, makes it plain that it was a case of a last attempt by the Etruscans to block the way and prevent the Romans from pressing on up the Tiber to Perugia or through the fertile Paglia-Chiana valley past Orvieto to Chiusi and Cortona. The importance to-day of the railway station of Orte as a junction on the Florence–Rome line enables us to understand the role which Lake Vadimon played in the struggles for Etruria after the Romans had succeeded in by-passing the barrier formed by Sutri, Nepi and Città Castellana (Falerii).

4. THE GREAT CALL-UP

The Battle by Lake Vadimon, 308 B.C.

By means of a '*lex sacrata*', a law promulgated in the name of the gods, says Livy, the Etruscans called up an army of such size and valour as they had not hitherto brought together. When it is further explained that this consisted in each man recruiting the next, it will be seen that this was a sort of snowball system, by means of which the great men of the country collected a following around themselves through their personal connexions, and the members of this retinue for their part attracted to themselves acquaintances and friends whom they deemed to be doughty and reliable. This appears to be evidence of an extremely ancient and interesting sort of militia formation, which differs profoundly and radically from the Roman conscription of citizens as also from a fighting unit composed of tribal groups.

Fig. 38. Warrior's tombstone from Vetulonia, the so-called Avle Feluske stele, seventh century B.C. Height 39⅝ in.

No doubt the activities of the roving warrior princes typical of earlier Etruria, such as Porsenna, or the brothers Vibenna, were also based on this manner of forming a following, as were those of Hirumina from Perugia who set up in Vetulonia to a comrade in arms the *stele* with the oldest known inscription of them all (Fig. 38) bearing the name of Avle Feluske. Is it possible that the mention of the *lex sacrata* in this connexion means that it was not so much a question of a call-up or of action by the cities themselves, as of a summons to the Voltumna priesthood, wherefore the ancient recruiting system described took the place of normal levying of troops? This would once again underline the political and military autonomy and independence of the cities allied in the Confederation. It has also to be seen in the light of what we otherwise know from Roman and Greek history of the distinction between national and private wars.[1] In this army, created by the *lex sacrata* and by one man recruiting another, citizens from Perugia, Chiusi or Tarquinii could serve against Rome when their own city actually had a truce or even a certain degree of friendly alliance with Rome.

In this battle Romans and Etruscans went for each other with such ferocity that it was by no means a mere exchange of spears or lances. With naked sword each man launched himself upon his opponent and war fever rose to an increasing pitch 'so that the Romans imagined they were not fighting with the Etruscans they had so often conquered but with some new race.' Row upon row of fighters fell, till ultimately the Roman cavalry dismounted from their horses and pressed forward on foot over fallen men and arms strewn around. This intervention of fresh untired forces decided the battle. The foremost Etruscans turned and thereupon all took to wild flight. 'On this day' says the report, 'was broken for the first time the power of the Etruscans, made mighty through long prosperity. The main part of their troops fell in the battle, their camp was taken by storm and plundered.'

Scarcely a generation later, in the year 283 B.C., another important battle took place in the same area round Lake Vadimon. On this occasion the Romans were opposed simultaneously by the Etruscans and the Gallic tribe of the Boii who were at that time their allies, and who had set out on the road to Rome, as once the Semnones had done. Once again the Romans were victorious. Scarcely a single one of the Gauls

[1]Cf. p. 139.

escaped and the Tiber flowed red from the blood of the fallen Etruscans.

Quintus Fabius is said to have pressed on to Perugia immediately after the first battle of Lake Vadimon in order to profit by his victory and to punish the city for having broken the truce. Those who opposed him were swiftly overthrown and soon the Roman army stood under the ramparts of the city, which immediately surrendered. Its citizens had to send emissaries to beg for peace from the Roman senate and had to declare themselves willing to receive a Roman garrison. It was this that caused the Etruscans to permit their language to be driven out so surprisingly quickly by the Roman tongue even from the burial urns.

The Defeat of Rusellae

In the year 303 B.C. another big battle with the Etruscans was fought, this time in the neighbourhood of the place to-day called Grosseto, which lies beneath the walls of Rusellae, still impressive even in their ruined state. In describing the outcome of this encounter Livy uses almost the same words with which he describes the result of the first battle by Lake Vadimon: 'With this battle the military power of the Etruscans was broken for the second time.' This formula of Livy's permits us to conclude that here again the Confederation as such had assembled an army on the basis of one man recruiting another throughout the whole of Etruria.

The conclusion of a forty-year truce with Tarquinii as a consequence of the Vadimon victory had laid open to the Roman armies the way into the western coastal areas of Etruria, which had been blocked for so long. Now, after the battle of Rusellae, the wealthy ore-bearing country of the north, the hinterland of Vetulonia, Populonia and Volterra, lay exposed to the clutch of the legions.

This battle had been preceded by an attempt on the part of the Tuscans to entice a section of the army led by the dictator Marcus Valerius Maximus into a widely spread ambush, a smaller operation of this type having on a previous occasion led successfully to the shameful defeat of a formation of Roman troops. The alarm in Rome over this defeat had been as great 'as if the whole army had been annihilated'. A judicial moratorium was proclaimed, sentinels were placed at the gates and in the streets, and defensive weapons set up on the ramparts.

Light is thrown on the language position among the Etruscans by

Livy's account of this incident, according to which the Roman commander recognized the enemy's new attempt at deception because of their manner of speech. Behind the blackened ruins of a burned-down village, not far from the Roman camp, the Tuscans concealed armed troops. Then they drove a herd of cattle past, to tempt the Romans to make a sally. When the Romans did not move, however, one of the drovers came close under the earthworks surrounding the camp and called to the others who were rather hesitantly driving their cattle out towards the camp from the tumbledown village, that they ought not to hang back so, they could drive their beasts safely through the Roman camp.

People from Cerveteri translated to the deputy-commander who was in charge what the man had said. He instructed them to note whether these herdsmen spoke with an accent of the towns or more like country people. The accent, the bearing and the smart outward appearance were too refined for herdsmen, they told him, and he now, for his part, let the disguised men be informed that their machinations had been discovered, and that they should no longer believe they could conquer the Romans through cunning or through force of arms. The battle, so fateful for the Etruscans, then began.

5. WEAKENING BY SOCIAL STRUGGLES

Civil War in Arezzo

This war, which after a successful beginning terminated in such a decisive defeat for the Etruscan army, is said to have been started by an uprising of the plebs against the family of the Cilnii who had ruled since olden times in Arretium. Driven out of their city by force this family received help, not, strangely enough, from the Voltumna Confederation but from the Romans. This makes it seem possible they were the guarantors of that obviously unpopular thirty-year truce with Rome, which Arezzo like Perugia and Cortona had concluded in the year of the first Vadimon battle. The very ancient royal family from which the great Maecenas later sprang, is here mentioned for the first time. After the victory at Rusellae the family was restored by the Roman dictator to its former position in Arezzo.

For the first time too we see here plainly that the same bitter tensions and dissensions between plebs and patricians which disturbed the Roman state for centuries and which at times brought it virtually to the brink of disaster, were also present in the cities of the Confederation of the Twelve and in fact crippled and split its forces just when an opponent such as Rome and the repulse of the Gallic hordes required the united and unanimous intervention of all classes.

Similar discords seem to be indicated by the report dating from the year 300 B.C. to the effect that the Etruscans had then publicly censured their great men in their assemblies for not having drawn the Gauls into the Roman war, on no matter what terms.

The Fall of Volsinii

This internal disunity was in fact to lead directly to the fall of the city of Volsinii, in whose territory lay the central Etruscan shrine, and which perhaps on that account offered the longest and toughest resistance to Rome of all the cities of the Etruscans. The last Etruscan victory by a Roman commander of which we hear was that over Volsinii and the city allied with it, Vulci. This was in the year 280 B.C., and the victor *de Vulsiniensibus et Vulcientibus*—over the Volsinians and the Vulcientians—was, as inscriptions show us, the consul Tiberius Coruncanius. In the course of the conflict the leading families of Volsinii had found themselves compelled to arm their bondsmen and lead them into the field and in return had had to make one concession after another to them. The bondsmen acquired active and passive voting rights, a seat in the senate, the right of inheritance and even the right to woo patricians' daughters. These developments may have taken place over a longer period of time than appears from the reports, and it is also possible that the class climbing upwards in society may have been plebs rather than slaves.

However, it is evident that after the defeat of 280 B.C., the situation became so tense that the leading families turned to Rome for aid, as the Cilnii had done in Arezzo. Somehow the people learned of this secretly initiated attempt. There was a furious outburst of a kind which in Rome was so often narrowly averted, either by luck or by the skill and reputation of individuals. The rebels seized power and took cruel revenge on those who had been their rulers till then, for injustices actually and allegedly suffered. They took their wives for themselves and placed the daughters of the nobles under the *jus primae noctis*, while all their former masters on whom they could lay hands were tortured to death.

The Romans profited by this opportunity to intervene, and figured, here as in Arezzo, as the defenders of the patrician system. After a long drawn-out siege hunger finally forced the rebels to surrender. They were executed as mutinous slaves or handed over for punishment to those of their opponents who survived. The city itself was razed to the ground, the remainder of the population being resettled elsewhere, right on the shore of the lake. The Bolsena of to-day grew from this once insignificant place.

These events show how both Rome and the Etruscan cities had to deal with similar social problems and how fatefully and fundamentally the two peoples were linked to one another despite all their quarrels. This was not a war between separate countries but rather a struggle for the unification of Central Italy. Central Italy was in those centuries an area which was culturally relatively homogeneous but politically still split up into numerous individual city-states, each retaining its autonomy as a basic religious element of its existence. Tuscan thinking was firmly established in the *Disciplina Etrusca*: in the works of art of the Tuscans we can trace how they were anchored to the conceptions of preclassical times. They could not but be at a disadvantage compared with Rome, whose outlook was far more realistic.

6. UNIFICATION WITH ROME

Economic Collapse

In Cerveteri the tendency to come to terms with the aspiring power on the Tiber and to tolerate certain restrictions on its part was early visible. A similar attitude can be traced throughout Etruria from the time of the first battle beside Lake Vadimon and it was the leading families who were showing most signs of readiness to do this. Just as Rome bought Brennus off, so the Etruscan cities began to buy off the Gauls through tributes of gold or goods and even to purchase freedom from the constantly repeated Roman invasions. The amount of money paid out in this way was so great that it was sufficient to maintain temporarily considerable sections of the Roman army.

It is not easy to find the reasons for such unwarlike behaviour, for many witnesses describe these people as inherently brave and scornful of death. Possibly a considerable role was played by the progressive loss, as a consequence of the troubles of a war lasting for decades, of the sources of wealth on which rested the supremacy of the *lucumo* and patrician families. It was not only trade which had to suffer: the Romans for a time waged the war extensively and systematically 'more with the land than with men' and 'by scorching and burning'.

'The obstinacy of the Faliscans and Tarquinians' says Livy in his account of the year 351 B.C. 'was overcome so completely by debilitation as by the wasting of a lingering illness, that they begged first the consuls and then, with their permission, the senate for a truce, which was granted to them for forty years.'

Simultaneously with the disappearance of the economic bases of the social system which had hitherto prevailed, a direct process of dissolution was going on through the growing pressure to extend the military call-up and to send into battle classes who had hitherto seldom or never been called upon to do service under arms. That this inevitably involved concessions in the form of social rights is clearly shown by the case of Volsinii, and developments in Rome itself offer plenty of illustrative material of the same process.

If one adds to this what has been said about the religious foundations of the existence of the Etruscan city and about the significance of the *Disciplina Etrusca*, and if one remembers how bitterly disputed in Rome was the question whether a man from a non-patrician family could read the signs of the gods, or perform scrutinies of birds and sacrifices, then one begins to appreciate to some extent the awkward situation of the Etruscan ruling classes. Faced with the choice—put in many different forms—between political independence and continued existence of the old religious organization, they finally decided in favour of the latter at least so far and so long as no other solution presented itself. The doctrine of the *saecula* which held out a prospect of the end of the *Nomen Etruscum* in the near future, and that fatalism which accepted the possibility of a short postponement of destined events but not of their alteration, probably clinched matters. Because these people directed all their thoughts towards the powers of the underworld, towards death and the world beyond, their thoughts and actions could not be governed by events which took place in this world. For the same reason they also produced no written history in our sense of the term.

The Founding of Roman Colonies

The main object of the invasions of the Gauls had been to gain land which they could cultivate and on which they could settle. Now what had been refused to the demanding people from the north with such obstinacy and at the cost of considerable sacrifice in men's lives and money reserves, had to be granted to the Romans. First Sutrium had had to accept Latin settlers a hundred years earlier, in 383 B.C., then in the year 273 B.C. the maritime city Cosa, later called Ansedonia, grew up on the Tyrrhenian coast not far from Vulci on land forcibly seized from the Vulcientians. Its mighty walls, long held to be extremely ancient, and the platform substructure of the temple which once dominated the city on the isolated mountain, together with the considerable remains of baths, halls, houses and streets, bear witness to the spirit of enterprise and will to dominate with which the Romans proceeded here. The channels cut through the rocks and the tunnels which served to drain and render healthy the marshy lagoon of Burriano, situated a brief hour's journey to the south, and which facilitated the extension of its harbour, are immensely impressive. The view of this spot seen during the journey from Rome to Leghorn or indeed even a glance at the map makes it outstanding strategical position plain. So, making use of the natural division of the Tyrrhenian coast, this place became a sort of outpost which divided southern Etruria with Cerveteri, Tarquinii and Vulci, from the region of the northern cities Rusellae, Vetulonia, Populonia and Volterra, and at the same time offered a sheltered and commanding base to the Roman fleet on a coast which was on the whole poor in harbours.

The founding of Alsium in 247 B.C. and Fregenae in 245 B.C., in the coastal territory of Cerveteri, seem to have been followed soon after by the establishment a little further north of Castrum Novum and Pyrgi and show Rome taking the Tuscan coast firmly into her hands. There can be no more talk, even in their own waters, of the Etruscans commanding the sea. On Tarquinii's shore Graviscae arose in 181 B.C. and at the same time in the inland territory of Rusellae on the other side of the Albegna and above the medicinal hot sulphur springs the mountain hamlet Saturnia appears, which is still surrounded by considerable parts of its defensive walls and whose Etruscan predecessor or counterpart has left its traces behind in the tomb-chambers of Pian di Palma situated on the other bank.

The establishment of such colonies meant that the territory of the Etruscan cities affected was shrinking and that in their relations with Rome they were submitting to a restraint which must not be underestimated, yet their actual existence and their separate cultural and religious life was scarcely touched. Nothing suggests that the shrine of Voltumna had ceased to exist or had suffered any diminution in its significance or its esteem within Etruria. There does, however, seem to be a possibility that after the destruction of Volsinii the headquarters of the priesthood passed to Tarquinii, for inscriptions seem to indicate that appropriate colleges for priests were established there.

Romanization

It is difficult to trace the individual phases of the process of the Romanization of Etruria during the last two centuries of the Roman republic. It is not really so much a question of the Etruscans voluntarily or involuntarily adopting foreign ways of thought and customs, or even of the Indo-Germanization of Asiatics settled as strangers in European Italy, as is still frequently suggested to-day. The differences between the one place and the other were too slight and the cultural trend, despite all struggles for self-assertion or power, had for too long been in the opposite direction. It was rather that in the course of time a sort of natural leadership had devolved upon Rome which the Carthaginian wars had confirmed and her victories had greatly strengthened. As a result the other cities of Italy, including of course the Etruscan ones, quite incidentally acquired a provincial character which became more and more marked in proportion as Rome developed into the head of a world empire. We see Rome absorbing talents and ambitions and efficiency from every part of Italy into herself where, as in a hermetically sealed vessel, all the varied ingredients and elements are fused and formed into rays of light, which Rome then, by a process of refraction and reflection, projects back into her immediate and more distant surroundings.

The obligations and levies imposed seem to have varied in form and degree from case to case, for each city was treated by Rome as a separate partner. The usual relationship was obviously that of *civitas federata*, allied community. On the whole the bonds were so tolerable and so favourable for the continued existence of the Etruscan ruling families and the organizations connected with them that even as early as the time of the Punic Wars (264–146 B.C.) there were no more difficulties or revolts worth mentioning. True, Rome had to worry more than once about rumoured or genuine Etruscan conspiracies and threatened revolts, but the presence of Roman troops, the watchfulness of the senate and the firm and vigorous action taken in those isolated cases which did occur sufficed to ensure that loyalty was generally maintained.

Shortly before the beginning of the second Punic War the Gauls invaded Central Italy afresh with powerful armies and pressed on plundering and laying waste as far as Chiusi. At this time, when terror and fear were so great among the Romans that they did not shrink from burying alive two Gauls, a man and a woman, as sacrifices in the cattle market in fulfilment of an oracular pronouncement, the Etruscans allowed Rome to encounter alone the dreaded enemy, who had so often in the past been their ally or their foe. In the year 225 B.C. in a great double battle north of Cosa, near Telamon, the intruders were, despite their great number and savage bravery, overwhelmingly defeated by the consuls attacking simultaneously from north and south. Rome's position as Etruria's protecting power was thenceforth unquestioned.

Even when eight years later Hannibal inflicted the terrible defeat of Lake Trasimene on the Romans in the centre of Etruria, there was no question of an uprising or of an alliance with the Punic national enemy. On the other hand, in the year 205 B.C. when the younger Scipio Africanus set about crossing over to Africa, intending to seize boldly for himself the right to trade, Etruria stirred. Her wealth and her economic structure are manifested in the aid spontaneously vouchsafed. It is true that, in contrast to the Umbrians and Sabines, she did not give soldiers or ships' crews. But Cerveteri, Perugia, Chiusi, Rusellae, Volterra and Arezzo delivered grain; Tarquinii donated canvas for sails; Populonia iron; Cerveteri victuals in addition. Timber for shipbuilding was contributed also by Perugia, Chiusi and Rusellae; and Arezzo added to its 120,000 measures of wheat 3,000 each of helmets and shields, 50,000 javelins, arrows and spears and the total armament of axes, spades for trench digging, sickles, baskets and hand-mills needed for forty ships.

Roman Citizenship

The war of the confederates (90–88 B.C.) brought Roman citizenship to the Etruscans because they had not, apart from small isolated operations, participated in the revolt of the Italic people. This removed the last formal obstacle to amalgamation. They became thereby also increasingly involved in the internal dissensions of the Romans and they themselves regarded the year 88 B.C., connected with the name of Sulla, as being their last.

Sulla's victory over Marius did in fact rank as an important event in the history of Etruria, as he raged ruthlessly and bloodily against the Tuscan families who had unwisely ranged themselves on the side of his opponent in the civil war. Fiesole, Arezzo, Cortona, Volterra and Populonia had to pay dearly. His punitive expedition, his ruthless conduct and the fact that he introduced Roman colonists within their walls after breaking their resistance, thereby also preparing the way for a speedy mingling of the population, can indeed all be understood as consequences of the earlier acceptance of Roman citizenship. For Sulla's action was in fact directed primarily against Roman citizens and only secondarily against Etruscans.

Caesar and the Triumvirs continued in this path, which Augustus concluded when, as part of his administrative reforms, he constituted Etruria as *Regio VII* an independent administrative district, and allotted it its place within the empire without any special privileges. Propertius boasts of him that he let Perugia go up in flames and thus 'destroyed the hearth of the ancient original Etruscan race'.

Survival of Features of Etruscanism

Rome now became the political centre and Latin displaced Etruscan as the language of public communications and in inscriptions on stones. We do not know how far Etruscan survived as a religious language or even in formulae for worship. The Etruscan 'discipline' in any case continued to be fostered. Indeed in these last centuries it seems to have developed into that confusing complex, ranging from a magnificent passion for life to a collection of abstruse contradictions, which we encounter in the late and unfortunately almost sole written sources. This development seems to have been caused by speculations and the integration into the 'discipline' of every possible philosophical and mystical doctrine from every part of the Mediterranean region into which Hellenism penetrated. The Roman grammarians took an antiquarian interest in the Etruscan language and it appears that in Tarquinii itself a certain amount of codification was undertaken.

The extent to which Etruscan influence continued to be active is

even more difficult to ascertain than the processes of fixation and con-
servation which were being carried out in grammatic, philosophical
and theological writings, which have also come down to us only in
extracts, generally difficult to understand. Whenever soothsayers and
prophets are required the Roman emperors continue for centuries
to use the *haruspices*, who were organized into a sort of 'order'. Yet
there are two contradictory reports according to one of which the
Emperor Constantine on several occasions promulgated decrees against
the bringing in of Etruscan soothsayers to foretell the future, while
according to the other he restored to the festival in the grove of Voltumna its old character as the principal ceremony of the Etruscan Confederation by removing the Umbrian participants therefrom. The
Emperor Julian repealed the prohibition of forecasting the future;
Valentinian, Valens and Gratian permitted once again scrutiny of
entrails; while the Emperor Theodosius in A.D. 385 and again seven
years later, strictly prohibited every kind of haruspication. But Etruscan
lightning conjurers could still in the year A.D. 408 offer their assistance
to the Romans then threatened by Alaric, when the bishop of the city,
Innocent, permitted them to give a public display of their skill in
conjuring up lightning.

Evidently through all that time the old secret knowledge had been
kept alive and handed down from generation to generation. Its influence on the intellectual life of late ancient times, on alchemy, gnosis
and mystery-cults has been too little investigated for it to be possible to
make accurate statements on this point. We know still less of the course
of the progress of Christianization in Etruria, some of whose *lucumo-
nies* became bishoprics, e.g. Rusellae, Vulci, Orvieto. In ecclesiastical
representational art too there has been little research to ascertain the
extent to which enrichment and colouring accrued to the new doctrine
from this country which had always been receptive to eschatological[1]
products of the mind.

Maecenas stands before us as the image of an Etruscan of the late
period, the lively confidant of Augustus, interested in all the arts and
sciences and possessing a sure instinct. He was conscious of his lucu-
monian origin, and in contrast to Roman habit and Roman legal
custom scorned every official title. Yet he occupied such a powerful

---

[1]Eschatology = the doctrine of the last or final things, as death, judgment.
the state after death (translator's note).

and important position in public life that he had the right to use the Emperor's signet ring in the latter's absence, and to act for him. Virgil, with the surname Maro which corresponded to an Etrusco-Umbrian official title, the eminent authority on Tuscan doctrines and traditions and indeed on all ancient heritages in general, who is included in the spiritual fathers of the Occident, came from Mantua, the capital city of the former northern Etruscan Confederation, where even in his time the Etruscans still played a leading role.

Presented to us in Cicero's letters and studies is Cecina, his friend from Volterra, learned in the law, whose family crypt has been found near Volterra. The Emperor Claudius boasted of his Etruscan forefathers and himself composed a history of the Etruscans, alas! now vanished and the Emperor Caligula, following Etruscan custom, had his little daughter Drusilla laid on the breast of the sacred statue of the goddess Minerva, soon after her birth, with the prayer that the goddess might nourish the child and let her grow.[1] So Etruscan ideas seem to be completely and wholly integrated and operative in late ancient culture though we can no longer discern all the details. A wide field lies open to research. To undertake it will deepen our understanding of antiquity.

[1] In this connexion may also be mentioned the great significance which Tages acquired in the time of the Roman emperors, when he was regarded as Xθόνιος Ἑρμῆς and put on a par with the compiler of the *Hermetica* and could almost be named in the same breath as Pythagoras, Plato, Orpheus and the prophets.

Summary of the Story of Etruria and of the History of Etruscan Research

I. THE COUNTRY AND ITS CITIES

THE valleys of the Rivers Arno and Tiber, which follow the slopes of the central Italian Apennines, form a wide, flat curve whose open side in the west is bounded by the Tyrrhenian Sea. The area thus enclosed by waters—the two rivers and the sea—is not quite as large as Sicily. Here the culture of the Etruscans unfolded and flowered in the period which began at the end of the eighth and ended in the first century B.C. Their memory is preserved in the name Tuscany, land of the Tuscans, which embraces by far the greater part of the area.

The twelve cities which formed the Etruscan Confederation lay strung out along the natural lines of communication of the countryside. From north to south, high on the mountain tops bordering the fruitful vale of Chiana, which links the valleys of the Arno and Tiber, Arezzo, Cortona and Chiusi stand to-day as they used to above the Tiber. Then comes Perugia famed far and wide to-day for its university for foreigners, and its wealth of important art treasures, then Orvieto, Città Castellana and Veii, Rome's old rival. The journey from Rome back to the north along the seashore leads us past Cerveteri with its countless tumulus tombs, and Tarquinii famous for its coloured tomb-paintings, past Vulci, Rusellae, Vetulonia and Populonia. Further inland and almost as high as Arezzo, on the far side of the tawny waters of the River Cecina, lies Volterra the city which may perhaps formerly have counted among its possessions Populonia, the place where copper was smelted and transshipped.

The heart of the Etruscan Confederation was the sacred grove of Voltumna the 'greatest god of all the Etruscans', in the territory of Volsinii which gave its name to the silvery Lake Bolsena. The actual site of this shrine, so important for an understanding of Etruscanism, is to-day unknown despite the fact that it maintained its importance till as late as the days of Constantine the Great.

Scenically, ancient Etruria can be divided into two halves, the southern which includes parts of Latium and which takes its character from the conspicuous grey and reddish-yellow tuff-stone and the canyon-like ravines known as '*fossi*'; and the northern whose rivers are thick with sediment and which possesses the gentle contours formed by conglomerates and masses of sedimentary rocks. The tuff ridges near Orvieto towering up like the ruins of some gigantic rampart, and the city itself on its lofty island of rock falling steeply away round it, dominated impressively by its cathedral, tell the traveller from the north that he is entering the southern Etruscan countryside. Near the sea the division between north and south runs close to the former territory of the city of Vulci.

A specially attractive feature of this tuff landscape consists in the great lonely rock-tomb cemeteries of Bieda, San Giuliano, Norchia and Castel d'Asso in the area between Vetralla and Viterbo, and of Sovana, the barren birthplace of Pope Gregory VII situated not far from Pitigliano, the mountain city standing out picturesquely on the upper reaches of the River Fiora.

In addition to agricultural wealth and the formerly abundant forests and pastures, other important sources of Etruscan prosperity were the rich ore deposits in the Monti Metalliferi of Massa Marittima and on Elba, which were exploited particularly by Populonia and Volterra, and near La Tolfa, in the country lying behind Agylla (Cerveteri). Numerous warm and cold medicinal springs, sulphur baths, mineral waters and eruptions of steam containing boron indicate the volcanic character of this country which to this day is fairly frequently shaken by earthquakes.

In the course of the sixth century B.C. two additional Etruscan Confederations of twelve cities were formed, one to the north and one to the south of Etruria proper, one situated in the plain of the Po with its capital, Mantua, dedicated to Mantus the god of death, and one in the south embracing Campania as far as the River Sele in the plain of Salerno, whose capital was Capua. Pompeii is said also to have been Etruscan for a time.

Information about these Confederations is scanty, but they were evidently autonomous formations not dependent on Etruria itself. Unifying factors in all these areas which were, as was Etruria proper, inhabited by populations which generally showed little basic uniformity, were the religious doctrine known as the *Disciplina Etrusca* and the Etruscan script and language which appertained to it. The extent to which groups of emigrants from the cities of the Voltumna Confederation participated in establishing the other Confederations is uncertain. Felsina, predecessor of Bologna, and Marzabotto, which is situated close to it, have given us a first glimpse of the peculiar characteristics of northern Etruscan culture, and Spina, recently rediscovered in the flooded area of Comacchio, promises further welcome disclosures. The northern Confederation succumbed in the fourth century B.C. before the assault of tribes from Gaul while the southern one fell almost simultaneously to the Samnites.

Etruria proper suffered its first serious damage with the loss of Veii. This city, after a struggle which lasted for generations and whose outcome was frequently in the balance, was defeated in 396 B.C. by Rome, its neighbour, a city then waxing in strength. It was the first of the twelve Etruscan cities to fall and was transformed into arable and pasture land. Though Gallic hordes and Hannibal's armies marched through the rich fields of Etruria, plundering and levying tribute, she did not in the end fall to them but to Rome which, from the date of the victory over Veii, gradually bound Etruria piece by piece to her by means of ruthlessly waged wars, treaties and colonization.

2. MUSEUMS

There is scarcely one of the museums of Etruscan antiquities which does not also possess great numbers of Greek monuments of art of different periods, especially vases, among which are to be found famous pieces of inestimable value for an understanding of Greek painting and culture. These came from Etruscan tombs as indeed do the majority of Hellenic vessels exhibited in Europe and in overseas collections. He who would understand Etruria must not fail to take account of them. It should be remembered that though they are of Greek origin they were after all for centuries the normal possessions of Etruscans and it is from the Etruscans that we have inherited them. It is essential to appreciate and to bear in mind that one of the distinguishing characteristics of the Etruscans was a readiness to adopt all that was Greek, especially Archaic and Late Greek, in the same way as we regard Hellas as one of the roots of our own culture. When we realize this, then what is peculiarly and unmistakably Etruscan stands out all the more plainly.

In the extensive Archaeological Museum in Florence we can get an idea of the diversity of the treasures found in Etruscan tombs, ranging from the Early Iron Age down to the period of Late Hellenism. Here we can also obtain a picture of the marked individuality of the different city-states and observe the process of fusion which went on somewhat hesitantly within the Confederation of the Twelve but which was never brought to completion. In this museum the positively overwhelming quantity of articles discovered is displayed in hall after hall, according to a strictly topographical system of arrangement. Original tomb-structures from every part of the country have been brought to the Archaeological Garden belonging to this museum—urn-tombs, tomb-chambers and tomb-tumuli—so that an insight into the science of Etruscan tombs can be obtained in a very small space.

In the *Villa Giulia* in Rome the most modern display technique has been used to exhibit a collection consisting of magnificent objects care-fully selected from the large number of mainly southern Etruscan treasures housed there. Its highlights are the archaic terracotta plastics from Veii which were only discovered during the last twenty years. The nucleus of the *Museo Etrusco Gregoriano*, the Etruscan Museum of the Vatican, is the collection of precious relics from the *Tomba Regolini-Galassi* in Cerveteri, while their counterparts from the Barberini Tomb in Praeneste are shown in the city's *Museo Preistorico ed Etnografico* in the *Collegio Romano*.

A visit to the *Museo Civico* of Bologna is of great assistance to an understanding of the Villanova culture of the Early Iron Age which marks the beginning of the evolution of Etruscan culture. This museum also contains a large number of interesting sculptured tomb *stelae* dating from the immediately following centuries. A visit should also be paid to the *Museo Preistorico dell'Italia Centrale* in Perugia, with which is combined the former Etrusco-Roman Museum and which is very clearly arranged; and to the museum in the *Palazzo Vitelleschi* in Tarquinii, famous for its sculptured sarcophagi.

Among the numerous local collections, both public and private, which the traveller can easily find, mention must be made of the small but comprehensive museum of Chiusi with its chair *canopi* in human form, the strange figure vases and archaic tomb *cippi*, an essential complement to which is the Casuccini Collection (removed to Palermo); and the *Museo Guarnacci* in Volterra, where the galleries and corridors are full of limestone and alabaster urns of the third to the first century B.C., decorated with illustrations in relief, examples of Hellenism in Etruria. There is scarcely a single archaeological collection in Europe or America which is without Etruscan antiquities. In Germany the most important museums are those in Berlin, some of whose items are still in store (since the war) in Wiesbaden and Celle; the *Staatliche Antikensammlungen* (the State Collections of Antique Art) in Munich containing the collections formerly belonging to King Ludwig I of Bavaria (*Wittelsbacher Ausgleichsfonds*, i.e. Wittelsbach Foundation); and the museum of the province of Baden in Karlsruhe for its Etruscan gold ornaments.

3. THE HISTORY OF ETRUSCAN RESEARCH

In Antiquity

Etruria was too closely linked with Rome's origins and with the history of Rome's rise to power not to have attracted the attention in ancient times of both Romans and Greeks interested in Rome's past. Of significant influence was *Archaiologia*, by Dionysius of Halicarnassus, the Greek *rhetor* and historian who lived in Rome in the time of the Emperor Augustus, in particular the six chapters of the first book of this work, devoted to the question of the origin of the Etruscans. Contrary to the story related by Herodotus of an immigration of Lydians across the seas from Asia Minor in legendary times, Dionysius is inclined to regard the Etruscans as an indigenous Italic population calling themselves *Rasenna*.

Dionysius of Halicarnassus became with this version of his the initiator of the flood of arguments on the question of origin which have occupied a central position in Etruscan research down to the present day and have, through the over-emphasis attached to them, made it more difficult to form an appreciation of Etruscan culture. At the end of the fifth century B.C. Hellanicus expressed the opinion that the Etruscans were a branch of the original pre-Greek Pelasgian population of the Aegean area. In later times theories of an immigration by land from the north over the passes of the Eastern Alps and from the northern Balkans over the Adriatic were propounded.

In most recent times, however, the view that these arguments are unfruitful has been held by ever increasing numbers of students and a new starting point has been adopted: viz. an appreciation of Etruscan culture for its own sake as something created and evolved in Etruria itself during the first millenium B.C. when there was much immigration of small and large groups, which mingled with the established population.

Much information about Etruscan organization and customs is also found in the writings of Livy, contemporary of Dionysius of Halicarnassus, and the Emperor Claudius is alleged also to have written a book on Etruscology called *Tyrrhenika*. Vitruvius describes the Tuscan temple as a typical structure of his time and Cicero deals with the Etruscan art of soothsaying. Servius, writing his annotations to Virgil in the fifth century A.D. could, when dealing with Etruscan matters, refer to a quantity of observations made by learned men on the antiquities and the language.

With the rise of humanism and the Renaissance the whole subject began to come to the forefront again and when K. O. Müller conceived and wrote his book on the Etruscans, a book whose basic significance can still be regarded as unchallenged and for which he received in 1826 a prize from the *Königliche Preussische Akademie der Wissenschaften* (Royal Prussian Academy of Sciences) in Berlin, the amount of information handed down by the ancient authors was, though fragmentary, so large that he alluded to monuments more to confirm than to correct what those ancient authors wrote.

In the Seventeenth and Eighteenth Centuries

It is surely one of the most fascinating facts in the historical evolution of the West that it was in Etruria that the Renaissance found its centre, the very area which once before, during the last thousand years before Christ, had pursued such fruitful contacts with Hellas. Thus the newly awakened interest in the study of the ancient world became in the most natural way an interest in the study of the Etruscans, and the more the soil yielded by way of monuments and information the more this was emphasized. For the time being Greece itself lay beyond the ken of the scholars: Rome and Etruria were laid bare.

Thomas Dempster (died 1625) was a Scot learned in law who was active at the University of Pisa and chose to make Italy his home. When, at the beginning of the seventeenth century he compiled a two-volume work called *De Etruria Regali* in which he put together all he had been able to get hold of in the writings of the ancients on old Etruria, he did not do this in order to stress the peculiarities or the uniqueness of the Etruscans as compared with other peoples of ancient times but rather in order to open up a broader approach to antiquity, respected by all scholars, than would have been possible through Rome alone.

This work did not appear until nearly one hundred years after his death, when Thomas Coke published it in 1723, but it had great influence then for it was just at that time that twelve enthusiastic scientifically-minded patrician citizens of Cortona united to form the *Academia Etrusca* in order that they might by their combined efforts collect a comprehensive library of the sciences of antiquity and carry out and foster research work into the past of their own country. It is noteworthy that they gave their president the ancient Etruscan royal title of '*Lucumo*'. No less a one than Johann Joachim Winckelmann applied in 1759 for membership of this somewhat exclusive society of learned men which 'for a whole generation has been the centre of all archaeological traffic and in its dissertations brings together the names of all the outstanding Italians and foreigners in the science of antiquity'. (Justi.)

In 1737–43 there appeared an item of great influence, the three-volume *Museum Etruscum, exhibens insignia veterum Etruscorum monumenta* a work with 300 copper engraving plates by Antonio Francesco Gori (1691–1757), who thus made accessible to educated people in all the countries of Europe those of Italy's antiquities which came from Etruscan soil. He produced three other books on the same lines— *Musei Guarnacci antiqua monumenta*, *Museum Cortonense* and *Museum Florentinum*. He thus laid a solid foundation for further study of these monuments by enthusiasts and research workers.

The publication of the work of Dempster, and of Gori's *Museum Etruscum* and the foundation of the *Academia Etrusca* are symptoms of a growing expansion of the science of archaeology, but we can trace another stimulus in the forefront viz. that national pride which regards the Etruscans as forefathers and makes a man seek in the representation of the glorious past the sign of ancient nobility for himself. In addition to the universal service which it had from the outset performed to the knowledge of antiquity, Etruscology became for many Italians in particular a national science, contributing to the awakening and growth of an Italian national consciousness and ultimately, when a united Italy came into being, it played a considerable part in the creation of the Italian kingdom and of a new Italian sense of mission. It is unnecessary to underline the dangers, as well as the inspiration which such an attitude gave and still gives rise to.

Like all studies of antiquity Etruscan research received decisive impetus from the influence of Winckelmann (1717–86). It is important to realize that in that period even he did not yet know how to distinguish Etruscan from Greek, though he did indeed strive to make this very distinction. Nevertheless Winckelmann made a vital contribution to scholarship by concentrating on the changing styles which must be taken into account when considering Etruscan art.

The Etruscan Language

It was only natural that the development of Etruscan research towards the idea of something self-contained should start first and foremost where the uniqueness of the material offered for investigation was from the very beginning indisputable, namely in research into the traces of the language. In 1789 there had already appeared the *Saggio di una lingua etrusca* of Luigi Antonio Lanzi (1732–1810), the third volume of which presented about five hundred Etruscan inscriptions with translations and commentaries.

In this 'Story of an Etruscan Language' he laid the foundation for the *Corpus Inscriptionum Italicarum* which was published approximately eighty years later in 1867 by Ariodante Fabretti and which was followed in 1893 by the *Corpus Inscriptionum Etruscarum* published jointly by the Academies of Science of Berlin and Leipzig.

General progress in the field of linguistics was made in 1822 by the deciphering of Egyptian hieroglyphics by François Champollion and in 1833–52 by Franz Bopp in his *Vergleichende Grammatik*, 'Comparative Grammar'. But the most decisive assistance which research workers received was the discovery of a few Etruscan written memorials of smaller size such as the mummy wrappings of Zagreb already discovered in Egypt in 1848/9 but only recognized as Etruscan by J. Krall in 1892, and the clay tile of Capua found in 1899.

Luigi Lanzi in his interpretation of Etruscan inscriptions still relied essentially on similarity of sounds with Latin and Greek, but with

Fabretti begins a systematic attempt to arrive at an interpretation by means of studies undertaken on the monuments themselves and by 'combinations'. Thus he founded the so-called 'combination' method of Etruscology which has since led to substantial clarification, particularly of syntax and sense, whereas the so-called 'etymological' method which depends on word similarities has come to be regarded as less acceptable since it was discovered that among all the languages formerly spoken in the ancient Mediterranean area as far as the Caucasus there was scarcely one with which no links of origin could be traced by this method. Starting from the fact that Etruscan culture formed an inextricable part of the ancient world, comparisons have recently been made with the whole gamut of Latin forms of consecration, prayer and law and by this method and by statistical observations useful progress has been achieved.

Though much research remains yet to be done, it is safe to say that, so far as content and syntax are concerned, Etruscan inscriptions can be regarded as explained to such a degree that there is no question of counting any more on sensational revelations and also that from now on painstaking detailed work will be decisive. Since the language with all the contradictions, mixtures and adaptations which research has taught us to notice was obviously essentially complete at the time when Etruscanism began to take shape, the question of the origin of the elements composing it has ceased to be a key point for anyone who regards Etruscan culture as the result of a process of integration and formation taking place in Etruria itself. It has instead become a problem concerning the history of the prehistoric colonization of Italy.

In the Nineteenth Century

If we now look once again at Etruscan research as a whole, we see that the nineteenth century is remarkable firstly for an enormous increase in the number of monuments found, then for the improvement in travelling facilities and so in facilities for examining these monuments and lastly for the development of techniques of reproduction, including photography, by means of which the many new discoveries and the objects preserved in collections have been made accessible to ever wider circles.

In 1821–6 there appeared the six richly illustrated volumes of the *Monumenti Etruschi* of Francesco Inghirami, followed by the illustrated books of Domenico Valeriani (1833, Discoveries at Chiusi), of Guiseppe Micali (1769–1844) and of the architect Luigi Canina (1795–1856). The last named wandered up and down through every part of ancient Etruria and recorded with his draughtsman's pencil whatever he found in the countryside which he thought worthy of note in remains of tombs and buildings. Much that was thus recorded has long since fallen victim to decay, negligence, road-building and rational utilization of the soil.

Among the more important operations which have increased the number of monuments must be mentioned in particular the investigations of the tomb-chambers begun in 1827 in Tarquinii, from the much admired coloured paintings of which could be traced the history of ancient wall-painting from the seventh to the second century B.C.; and the excavations begun in 1828 by the Prince of Canino in the cemeteries of Vulci, which brought thousands of vases into the museums of Europe.

The great contribution made by Gustav Kramer to Etruscan research in his work *Styl und Herkunft der bemalten griechischen Thongefässe*[1] which appeared in 1837 was that he demonstrated the Greek character of these vases and so laid the first firm foundation for the idea that Etruscan art was something distinct and different from Greek art, although in his book interest is directed more towards a knowledge of Greek than of Etruscan works of art.

Mention must be made of a typical excavator of this time, Alessandro François, the discoverer of the *Tomba François*, in Vulci (1857), and of the so-called François bowl from Chiusi (1844) made by Clitias and Ergotimos, and now in the Archaeological Museum in Florence. In him we can see many features typical of his age, namely, scientific ardour, the archaeologist's passion for following a scent and treasure-hunting for profit.

In London there was published in 1848 the first edition of 'The Cities and Cemeteries of Etruria', a two-volume travel book by an Englishman, George Dennis, which combines, in a way not since achieved again, informative descriptions of monuments and places with a lively account of his experiences. Besides this work another proof of curiosity about Etruria at the time of Goethe is the book of the *Hofrat* Wilhelm Dorow published in Paris in 1829, *Voyage archéologique*

[1]'Style and Origin of painted Greek clay Vessels'.

dans l'ancienne Etrurie, and the travel book of Mrs. Hamilton Gray, published in 1840—'A Tour to the Sepulchres of Etruria in 1839'. Goethe himself took a lively interest in the wall-paintings which were coming to light in the Etruscan graves of Tarquinii during the last years of his life.

The foundation in 1829 of the *Instituto di Corrispondenza Archeologica* in Rome, made possible by the energy and devotion of Eduard Gerhard, stimulated a lasting interest in Etruscology. In this international society of learned men the important archaeologists and friends of antiquity of the day used to meet to study together and foster research. In the publications of this institute which were issued periodically, the *Annali dell'Instituto*, the *Bollettino degli Annali dell'Instituto* and finally the twelve large folio volumes of the *Monumenti inediti* (1829–85), Etruscan archaeology found its scientific home. Gerhard himself presented Etruscan research with a collective work, his treatise on mirrors (five Vols. 1843–97), in which he aimed at completeness, and which provides a basis for further study which is still so indispensable that we can easily forgive the fact that the drawn reproductions are in an old-fashioned style.

In Modern Times

The increase of public funds for archaeological research, the teaching of ancient history in high schools and the expansion of public art collections are expressions of the process which began in 1870. The *Instituto di Corrispondenza Archeologica* did not remain untouched as nationalism rapidly encroached on all aspects of life. In 1884 it surrendered its international character, being transformed—at first with some hesitation but later quite definitely—into the Rome branch of *das Deutsche Archäologische Reichsinstitut* (the German Archaeological Imperial Institute) while Italy, now a united independent kingdom, began to regard research and the excavation of the monuments remaining in its soil as a national duty.

An extremely valuable basic work which has appeared regularly since 1877 is the *Notizie degli scavi di antichità* in which the results of excavations in Italy are usually first recorded in outline. The evolution of Etruscology was significantly affected by a law for the protection of monuments, enacted in 1872 but based on long-established principles whereby all work of excavation was practically speaking reserved to

Italian research workers while archaeological research work by non-Italians was essentially confined to work on material already excavated. There were obviously dangers in such a division of labour but the wealth of publications and dissertations in countries where archaeology is pursued, which enabled Etruscan research to establish a place for itself within the science of antiquity, shows how these were overcome through loyalty and personal courtesy, through the overwhelming feeling of each that he was dependent on the other and the sense of unity felt in common activity and common enthusiasm.

In 1906–1909 appeared the studies of the Swede C. O. Thulin on the *Disciplina Etrusca*. With these volumes the study of religion began to develop as a special branch subject within Etruscology, as is indeed essential for the investigation of a culture whose chief characteristic in its time was held to be an unusual devotion to forms of worship and religion.

In 1927 Etruscan research ultimately acquired its own mouthpiece in the *Studi Etruschi*, the organ of the *Instituto di Studi Etruschi ed Italici*, which has its home in Florence and is maintained by the Italian state, while in the Universities of Rome and Florence there are now chairs for *Etruscologia e Archeologia Italica*.

Research by prehistorians has evolved new means of approaching the question of the origins of the Etruscans. Above all, however, the artists of the last decades have greatly facilitated a comprehension by people of our own times of expressions of art and life which, like many of the works of the Etruscans and like their peculiar religious ideas and doctrines, reject classical standards and which must be explained by the spiritual attitudes of that ancient people, which research is only just beginning to reveal to us.

SELECT BIBLIOGRAPHY

BOOKS TO READ ABOUT THE ETRUSCANS IN ENGLISH

THIS book was originally written in German. It contained a comprehensive bibliography and numerous footnotes throughout the text referred to published material on the Etruscans. Much of this material is in German or Italian, some in French or other languages, a little in English. Many of the publications are scientific or specialist journals not easily accessible. The list which follows consists of books available in English:—

Cambridge Ancient History (Cambridge University Press, 1926), especially: Vol. IV, Chapter XII, 'Italy in the Etruscan Age: A. The Etruscans', by R. S. Conway.

but also:

Vol. VII, Chapter XII, 'The Kings of Rome', by Hugh Last.

Vol. VIII, Chapter XIV, 'Rome: Religion and the Advent of Philosophy', by Cyril Bailey.

Vol. IX, Chapter XX, 'The Art of the Roman Republic', by Eugénie Strong.

Livy, Books V and VII particularly, but also Books I, II, IV, IX and X.

Tacitus, Annals XI (13, 14 and 15).

Polybius, II, 18–22; and VI, 53.

Cicero, De Divinatione, II, 23.

Seneca, *Quaestiones Naturales* ('Physical Science')—II, 32, 41 and 48.

Pliny, Natural History, II, 138–42.

Diodorus Siculus, XI, 88; XIV, 113–17; XV, 14; XIX, 106; XX, 11, 61 and 64; XXI, 3.

Sir William Gell, *The Topography of Rome and its Vicinity*, 2 vols. (Saunders & Otley, London, 1834).

Mrs. Hamilton Gray, *Tour to the Sepulchres of Etruria in 1839* (Hatchards London, 1840—2nd edn. 1841).

G. Dennis, *The Cities and Cemeteries of Etruria*, 2 vols. (John Murray, London, 1848, 3rd edn. 1883).

Mary Lovett Cameron, *Old Etruria and Modern Tuscany* (Methuen & Co., 1909).

Frederik Poulsen, *Etruscan Tomb Paintings—Their Subjects and Significance*, translated from the Danish by Ingeborg Andersen (Clarendon Press, Oxford. 1922).

R. A. L. Fell, *Etruria and Rome* (Cambridge University Press, 1924).

David Randall-MacIver, *The Etruscans* (Clarendon Press, Oxford, 1927).

Select Bibliography

D. H. Lawrence, *Etruscan Places* (Martin Secker, London, 1932).

J. D. Beazley, *Etruscan Vase-Painting* (Clarendon Press, Oxford, 1947).

M. Pallottino, *Etruscan Painting*, book of illustrations, all in colour, with text translated from the Italian by M. E. Stanley and Stuart Gilbert (Éditions, Albert Skira, Geneva, 1952).

M. Pallottino, *The Etruscans*, translated from the Italian by J. Cremona (Penguin, 1955).

M. Pallottino and H. & J. Jucker, *Art of the Etruscans*, book of illustrations with text translated from the Italian (Thames & Hudson, London, and Atlantis Verlag, Zürich, 1955).

Sibylle von Cles-Reden, *The Buried People*, translated from the German by C. M. Woodhouse (Rupert Hart-Davis, 1955).

Raymond Bloch, *The Etruscans*, translated from the French by Stuart Hood (Thames & Hudson, London, 1958).

INDEX

Note: The following terms appear so frequently in the text that they have not been included in the Index: Greece (Hellas), Greek (Hellene, Hellenic), Rome, Roman, Italy, Italic, Italian. The reader will, however, find in the index Athens, Corinth, Hellenism, and Latium.

When a page number appears in italic, the entry refers to a text illustration.

Index

Index

Conservators, Palace of the, Rome, *see* Museums (Italy) (Rome), Palazzo dei Conservatori

Constantine, the Emperor, 171, 174

Conway, R. S., 185

Copper, 16, 21, 66, 69, 93, 112, 173

Corcyra (Corfu), 119, 122

Corinth, Corinthian, Proto-Corinthian, 76–77, 102, 103, 104, 107, 108, 117, 118, 119, 122

Corpses, inhumation of, cremation of, *see* Burial Customs

Corsica, 119, 120, 121, 136

Cortona, 2, 3, 39, 50, 84, 153, 155, 159, 163, 170, 173, 179

Cosa (Ansedonia), 167, 169

Cossus, Aulus Cornelius, 130

Crete, 52, 88, 89, 119. *See also* Minos, Minoan

Croesus, 29

Cronos, 17, 20

Crotona, 50

Cumae, 34, 35 n., 76, 118, 119, 131–2, 133, 134

Cypselus, 117, 118

Cyprus, 68, 108

Dancing, 5–6, *6*, 99, 131

Danube Area, Danubian Cultures, 38, 52–55, 66, 68. *See also* Hallstatt, Lausitz

Death, 1, 5, 14, 25, 26, 55, 58, 60, 85, 98, 101, 166, 171. *See also* Demons

Delos, Delian, 40, 121

Delphi, 40, 120, 124, 125, 142, 144, 147

Demaratus, 117–18

Demon of Death, 75, *123*, *143*, of the Underworld, 25, 122, 145

Dempster, Thomas, 178, 179

Dennis, George, 3, 182, 185

Diana, Plate XVI

Di Consentes, 19, 128

Diodorus Siculus, 185

Dionysius of Halicarnassus, 32, 177 178

Dionysius of Syracuse, 135

Dionysus, *see* Fufluns

Discipline, The Etruscan (Disciplina Etrusca), 13, 20, 21, 41–43, 143, 152, 165, 166, 170, 175, 184. *See also* Tagetic Doctrine

Doctrine, Tagetic, *see* Tagetic Doctrine, Discipline; of the Saecula, *see* Saecula

Dorow, 47, 182

Dörpfeld, Wilhelm, 67

Drainage and Irrigation of Land, 3, 141, 144, 167

Earthenware, *see* Ceramics

Egypt, Egyptian, 9, 37, 53, 68, 71, 72, 98, 108, 116, 180

Eita, 99

Elba, 2, 4, 134, 136, 174

Emperors, Empire (Roman), 14, 31, 171, 172, 174, 178. *See also* Augustus, Caesar (Gaius Julius), Caligula Claudius, Constantine, Gratian, Julian, Theodosius, Valens, Valentinian

Epics, Greek, 1, 31, 80, 88, 104. *See also* Homer, Iliad, Odyssey

Ergotimos, 182

Etruscology, Etruscologists, 8 n., 33, 37, 70, 178, 179, 181, 183, 184

Eucheir, 118

Eugrammos, 118

Fabius, Marcus, 158

Fabius, Quintus, 139, 158, 159, 162

Fabretti, A., 180, 181

Faïence, 71, 72

Falerii, *see* Città Castellana

Faliscan, 3 n., 38, 166

Family Graves, 85–88, 91

Fate or destiny, belief in, 1, 12, 13–20, 27, 111, 142–5, 166; books of (*libri fatales*), 143; goddess of, 110, *and see* Nortia, Fortuna; nails of: *see* Nails

Fell, R. A. L., 185

Fibulae, 45, 71, 108, *109*, 111, 114–16, *115*, Plate XIVa

Fiesole, 2, 39, 153, 170

Fire, Significance of, 11, 12, 25, 57–58, 103, 110. For Cremation *see* Burial Customs

Florence, 1, *2*, 2, 52, 80, 82, 99, 117 151, 159, 176, 184. *See also* Museums

Formello, 34, 77

Fortuna (Chance), 12, 15, 27. *See also* Fate, Nortia

Founding Cities, 23–24, 41, 42, 64, 118, 151, 166

Index

96 n., 147, 176, Palazzo dei Conservatori, 77, *78*, *79*, 96, Pigorini-Museum, *73*, 74 n., Vatican Museums, 3, 45, 91–95, 100, 101, *103*, *108*, *112*, *115*, 176, Plates VI, XIVa, Other, 176; *Tarquinii*, 71, 176; *Volterra*, 27, 28 n., 177, 179

Museums (Yugoslavia), *Zagreb*, 37, 180

Music, Plate II, 5–6, 99, 131

Mycenaean, 52, 81, 82, 88, 89

Mysia, 30, 118

Nails, year nails, 12, 13, 18, 40, 111; nails as ornamentation, 92, 110–11

Narcissus, 8

Nepete (Nepi), *2*, 157, 159

Norchia, *2*, *4*, 59, 174

Nortia, 12, 18, 40, 83. *See also* Fortuna, Fate

Numa Pompilius, 50

Nuraghe, 52

Odyssey, 31, 67, 107, 117, 128

Olympia, 9, 40, 95, 107, 131, *131*, 134

Omphale, 30

Ore, incidence of and trade in, 4, 66–67, 76, 140, 162, 174. *See also* Copper, Iron

Orientalizing Style, Period, 67–74, 80, 81, 85, 91, 94, 98, 99, 102, 107, 112, 117

Origin of Etruscans, 7, 27–33, 177

Orpheus, 51, 172 n.

Orphism, 42, 49–51

Orte, 157, 159

Orvieto, *2*, *4*, 39, 70, 82, 99, 153, 159, 171, 173, 174

Painting, *see* Art
  for Tomb-Painting, Wall-Painting, Murals, *see* Tomb
  for Vase-Painting, *see* Vases

Palestrina, *see* Praeneste

Pallottino, M., 186

Pausanias, 95

Pectorals (Breast-plates), 72, 111–14, *112*

Pelasgian, 117, 177

Peloponnesian, League, 40; War, 135–6

Perrin, B., 24

Persephone (Persipnei), 12, 99

Persia, Persians, 58, 119, 121, 132

Perugia, *2*, 3, 9, 27, 33, 35, 37, 39, 52, 86, 94, 155, 159, 161, 162, 163, 169, 170, 173, 176. *See also* Museums

Phayllos, 134

Phocaeans, 119–25, 132, 133

Phoenicians, 66, 67, 68, 69, 72, 74, 79, 98, 132, 136

Phrygia, Phrygian, 38, 68

Piacenza, 21, *22*, 152

Pietra Zannoni, *see* Zannoni

Pietrera, *see* Tombs

Pindar, 132

Piracy, Pirates, 3, 72, 78, 79, 119, 121, 124, 132, 134, 137

Pisa, 39, 178

Plato, 172 n.

Pliny the Elder, 185

Pliny the Younger, 35

Plutarch, 15, 24, 50

Po, the Plain of the, *2*, 150, 152–3

Pole Star, 23, 39

Polybius, 96–7, 156, 185

Polyphemus, 79

Pompeii, 174

Populonia, Plate XI, *2*, *4*, 33, 39, *55*, 60, 82, 88, 89, 94, 119, 121, 148, 155, 162, 167, 169, 170, 173, 174

Porsenna, 126, 128, 138, 151, 154, 161

Portraiture, Art of, 16, 27–29, *28*, 52, 106. *See also* Art

Poseidon Heliconius, 49

Pottery, *see* Ceramics

Poulsen, F., 185

Praeneste (Palestrina), 12, 72, *73*, 116, 155, 176

Priests, 15, 25, 28, 41, 42, 45, 46, 72, 113, 124, 131, 140, 147, 152, 161, 168. *See also* Haruspex, Lucumo

Priest-Kings, 40, 127–8. *See also* Lucumo

Propertius, 3, 170

Punic War, *see* Carthage

Pythagoras, 49–51, 172 n.

Pythagoreans, 49–51

Pythoness (of Delphi), 120, 124, 142, 144. *See also* Delphi

Randall-MacIver, D., 185

Regolini-Galassi, *see* Tombs

Rehm, A., 35 n.

Index

Tinia, 19, 20, 21, 25, 42, 116, 127, 128. *See also* Jupiter Zeus

Tolumnius, 128, 129

Tomb Chambers, *see also* Vaulting, 43, 61, 71, 84, 86, 88, 89, 90, 91, 99, 167, 176, 182, Plate X

Tombs (general), 2, 8, 14, 33, 37, 70, 72, 76, 77, Chap. IV (81–117,) 176, 182

Tombs (named), Barberini Tomb, 72, 176; Bernardini Tomb, 72, *73*; Bocchoris Tomb, 71–72, 76, 111; Banditaccia Cemetery, 93–96, Camucia Tomb, 84; Casal Marittima Tomb, 82–83, Plate X; Grotta Campana, 82, 101, 140, *146*; Monte Calvario of Castellina, 84; Pania Tomb, 80; Pietrera, 83, 84, 89, 119; Volumnia Tomb, 86; Tomba degli Auguri, 122, Plates III, IV; Tomba della Caccia e della Pesca, *125, 126, 151*; Tomba Calabresi, *103*; Tomba Campana, 95; Tomba delle Cinque Sedie, 96; Tomba del Colle, *130*; Tomba della Doganaccia, 84, 88; Tomba del Duce, 80; Tomba François, 122, 138, 182; Tomba Golina, 99; Tomba delle Leonesse, *6*; Tomba dell' Orco, *123, 143*; Tomba Regolini-Galassi, 72, 81–116, *90, 92, 108, 112, 115*, 128, 176; Tomba dei Rilievi, 101; Tomba degli Scudi e delle Sedie, 95, 96, 101, Plate XII; Tomba dei Vasi dipinti, *148*; Tomba del Vecchio, *28*

Tombs of Families or Couples, *see* Family Graves

Tomb Painting (Wall Painting), 3, 5, *6*, 25, *28*, 99, 122, *123, 125, 126, 130*, 138, 140, *143, 148, 151*, 173, 182, 183, 185

Tombstones, 5, 26, 58, 59, 63 n., 75, 83, 94. *See also* Stele

Tomb Types: Cupola (Domed) Tombs, 4, 33, 83, 88–89, 119, Plate XI; Rock Tombs, 4, 25, 26, 59, 81–84, *84*, 85, 87, 88, 157, 174; Stone Circle Tombs, 60, 72, 80; Tumulus (Mound) Tombs, 3, 25, 82, 84–85, 86, 89, 91, 92, 93, 94, 102, 117, 128, 173, 176, Plate IX

Toreutics, 68–70. *See also* Metal-Working

Transformation, Transfiguration, Transsubstantiation, 1, 55, 58, 60, 64, 101, 102. *See also* Beyond, Death, Soul

Trasimene (Lake), 2, 169

Troy, 31, 52, 54, 122

Turan (Venus, Aphrodite), 11, 12, 13, 14, 19

Tuscania (Toscanella), 43, *44*, 47

Tyrrhenus (Tyrsenus), 30, 50

Ulysses, 31, 79, 117

Umbria, Umbrian, 30, 33, 35, 38, 158, 159, 169, 171, 172

Underworld, 1, 12, 24, 25, 75, 83, 99, 106, 122, 145, 166. *See also* Demons

Uni (Juno, Hera), 19, 145, 147–8, 154

Urns, Urn-Reliefs, 5, 8, 27, 28, 31, 33, 55, 56, 57, 58, *59*, 60, *61, 62*, 63, 65, 82, 84, 86, 87, 91, 93, 94, 101, 106, 110, 122, 162, 176, 177, Plate VIII. *See also* Canopic Jars, Helmet-Urns, Hut-Urns

Vadimon (Lake), 2, 159–62, 163, 165

Valens, the Emperor, 171

Valentinian, the Emperor, 171

Valeriani, D., 182

Valerius Maximus, 6

Valerius Maximus, Marcus, 162

Varro, 14

Vases, 8, 55, 67, 70, 71, 75, *76*, 88, 140, 175, 177, 182, 186. *See also* Bocchoris-Vase, Ceramics, Warrior Vase

Vatican, *see* Museums (Italy) (Rome)

Vaulting, Plate X, 81–89, 90

Vegoia (Begoia), 20, 42

Veii, Plate XV, 2, 3, 31, 34, 39, 57, 63, 77, 82, 101, 128, 129, 130, 137–49, *146*, 150, 151, 154, 155, 157, 173, 175, 176

Veiovis, 21

Veneti, 33, 155

Venus, *see* Turan

Vetulonia, Plate VIII, 2, 4, 39, 60, 61, 62, 63, 64, 72, 80, 82, 83, 84, 89, 94, 108, *109*, 119, 121, 155, *160*, 161, 167, 173

MIDLAND BOOKS